HEAR'S THE THING

HEAR'S THE THING

LESSONS ON LISTENING, LIFE, AND LOVE

CODY ALAN

HARPER HORIZON

Published by Harper Horizon, an imprint of HarperCollins Focus LLC.

Any internet addresses, phone numbers, or company or product information
printed in this book are offered as a resource and are not intended in any way to
be or to imply an endorsement by Harper Horizon, nor does Harper Horizon
vouch for the existence, content, or services of these sites, phone numbers, companies, or products beyond the life of this book.

Scripture quotations are taken from the King James Version. Public domain.

This is a work of nonfiction. The events and experiences detailed herein are all
true and have been faithfully rendered as remembered by the author, to the best
of his ability. Some names have been changed to protect the privacy of the individuals involved.

ISBN 978-0-7852-4929-0 (eBook)
ISBN 978-0-7852-4915-3 (HC)

Library of Congress Control Number: 2021939409

Printed in the United States of America
21 22 23 24 25   LSC   10 9 8 7 6 5 4 3 2 1

To Mom and Dad, with love.

• CONTENTS •

• FOREWORD •

THERE ARE PEOPLE IN YOUR life you don't recall meeting because it feels like they've always been there. That's where Cody Alan lives in mine. He's one of those people who you feel like you went to school with . . . heck, he *is* one of those people you went to school with: friendly, relatable, likable, easy to be around, easy to talk to. He's also one of those friends you have where, no matter how many weeks or months pass between seeing each other, you're able to pick right back up from where you left off, simply by saying, "So, anyway . . ."

What makes Cody so good as an interviewer is his ability to make you feel comfortable. Although I'm sure he's always well prepared, I never feel like he's thinking about his next question. There's always an authentic connection with him because he's totally present. He pays attention to someone's answer, then asks the next question within that answer. Cody is so easy to talk to that every one of our interviews feels like part of the same ongoing conversation about life, love, family, music. . . .

That comfort level stems from the fact that he knows how to listen. I mean *really listen*. Listening is imperative for growth, for connectivity, for being of service to someone else, for the creation of music and so much more. Sometimes listening is all that's required—but it's not necessarily as easy as Cody makes it look.

The ability to react openly to an environment or situation takes a kind of muscle memory, like a bird landing on a branch. It's a complex maneuver, and if he thought too hard about how he's going to land, he'd probably miss or crash into the tree trunk. In the same way, that listening muscle develops over a lifetime of caring and of having genuine curiosity about others.

To listen well you also need to slow everything down, to block out distractions and be in that moment, so the person you are speaking with is all there is. It requires patience to give someone the space they need to complete their thought and speak their truth. You need to be comfortable enough in those silences, those pauses, to enable the person you are listening to let out what needs to come out, without finishing their sentences or making assumptions.

To some degree, I think that level of patience is becoming a lost art because we don't get many situations to work on it. We have the instant ability to access many things that interest us, whether it's streaming music, surfing the web, going down rabbit holes on YouTube, or buying something online and having it delivered the next day. We've grown accustomed to instant gratification in so many areas of life that we've been deprived of the opportunity to learn patience. If you were to pray, "God, give me patience," it wouldn't just be given to you: you'd be put in a traffic jam or thrown into the line at the DMV! Patience must be learned.

A few years ago, I had the opportunity to practice patience and listening with Cody. We'd just finished an interview session and were catching up on each other's lives. I could hear in his voice that there was something significant he wanted to say to me. It was something personal, and I was deeply touched that he felt we were at a level of our friendship where he could confide in me. (Cody knows how seriously I take anonymity, and that I'd take anything he said to me to my grave.) I was also grateful that, with me, he knew he'd be understood, supported, and not judged in any way. I wanted to be a place of love and support for him, period.

Since then, Cody has gone on to reveal his truth to the world. He's become a major part of Nashville's growth as an inclusive community that is supportive of people as they seek to be their authentic selves.

What a great place to build from.

—Keith Urban

· INTRODUCTION ·

IT MIGHT SOUND WEIRD THAT a music and television personality who makes his living talking on air would write a book centered on how to shut up and let others speak. But I pride myself on being a professional listener in a world where no one hears each other anymore. Actively listening without judgment and showing empathy, making eye contact with the person you are speaking with, and mirroring their emotions can work miracles. While our social media screams "Look at me! Listen to me!" I've always loved hearing the stories of others. When someone feels heard, you're giving them permission to be their true, authentic self. I make my living getting country artists to open up about their lives, realizing that's where the best country music comes from: real life. And I'm able to do this because my listening skills have helped me establish a good rapport and sense of trust that allows them to be vulnerable, even when millions of people are listening!

This "superpower" has always been there. As a kid, I possessed natural curiosity and an empathy for other people. I asked questions, watched their reactions, paid attention to body language and to what was *not* said as much as what was. I was hypersensitive to how someone was feeling, and always zeroed in on people in the room who seemed awkward or unhappy, showing concern and asking friendly questions to draw them out of their shells. My mom used to call me her "ball of sunshine" because, even as a toddler, I'd do whatever it took to get someone to laugh or break into a smile.

I was also intensely nosy. Not in a mean or intrusive way. I just loved people and wanted to find out whatever I could to make a connection. Instinctively I knew just how far to probe or how much to share to make someone feel comfortable enough to open up to me. It was a skill that helped this kid win friends in school and throughout my life. That curiosity about others kept me rich in all kinds of relationships. And damn, I'm good at getting country artists to spill the tea!

But the one voice I wasn't listening to enough was my own. For years, I'd been deaf to my authentic self. I was a good listener to others in part because I was desperate to shut down the inner voice that was telling me who I truly was. There was always that invisible wall. As open as I may have seemed, my reluctance to let people in and share more of who I was limited how deep I could go. Ironically, being more willing to give to others has better equipped me to receive. I became a better listener, a better communicator, and a happier person when I finally flexed that compassionate listening muscle on myself.

And that's what this book is about: giving others, and yourself, permission to become their authentic selves by listening, understanding, and receiving with an open heart. It's time for a refresher course on the art of genuine listening that can help you build healthier relationships, deal with conflicts, improve understanding and accuracy, learn and discover new points of view, enhance your career . . . Anyone can attain great listening skills, but it takes constant practice.

I'm still a work in progress, and I've caught myself interrupting and making assumptions plenty of times. But the ability to really hear someone is a strength that's well worth honing, because improved hearing cascades into all areas of your life, whether you interview people for a living as I do, or you are just trying to build deeper connections with those in your life who matter most.

On these next pages, I'll share my story, along with the wisdom I've gathered along the way from some country music greats I've been privileged enough to meet and interview in depth. My intention is to use these experiences of listening and connecting with others to inspire you to open up more fully to all that the universe has to offer.

It's no coincidence that my passion is country music. These are the songs that tell a story. They were made for listening to with your full attention. That's why one of the catchphrases on my show is "Hear's the thing!" I want to make sure the audience is still there with me, catching every nuance. It's not just the music but the expression of the words that makes the record. You don't just tap your feet mindlessly and hum along to the hook while it plays in the background. You hang onto every line, feeling the emotion and intention of the artist who is singing. You lose yourself in the narrative and visualize the scene or the person who inspired those lyrics. In fact, a great country music song is the perfect training tool for listening with empathy. And, once you've gone country, you develop an ear for authenticity. You can feel what's real.

Against that backdrop, I'll share with you the various ways listening has played out in my life, from each step along the way toward exceeding my dreams of becoming a radio and TV host, to my personal growth as a husband, father, lover, and friend. You'll learn how paying attention to my inner voice made me clear about what I wanted to do in this life.

So that's what I'm offering you with this all-access pass to my world: a few snippets on the wisdom of listening from a country boy who may not be perfect but who always strives to do what's right. Consider this your invitation to share in my journey. I'm no expert, and I don't pretend to have all the answers, but I *can* offer you a few insights on the art of listening, and what's worked for me as I've fumbled my way toward becoming my true self. My goal is not so much to tell you how exactly to listen as to *show* how opening up my own ears has brought me my greatest joys. These insights come from a set of experiences and adventures on a road less traveled. But don't look for a set of prescriptions on these next pages. If you tune in and listen to my story, you will find your own takeaways. My desire above all is to entertain.

Consider this your invitation to listen in on my fun, crazy, and blessed life as a country music personality in Nashville. Throughout, you'll hear directly from friends and family, including my ex-wife Terresa's perspective on my coming out process, some behind-the-scenes memories with Keith Urban, my mom's memories of my childhood idiosyncrasies, and the entertaining insights of my closest friends in the industry. It seems only fair to allow you to hear my story through other voices and let them have their say!

Country music, which I consider one of my oldest friends, will be another recurring character in my story. I love listening to it with the windows down and the volume up. These artists are nothing but honest about the struggles of their lives, and increasingly I'm hearing a lot of compassion in their lyrics, so their warmth and kindness toward me stands to reason. I found plenty of comfort in this music when I went through some recent life-changing events. It gave me the courage to make an important leap of faith, which you'll learn about as you read on. When you fall, you might break a few bones, but embrace the pain, because it means you've fully lived. Own the joy *and* the suffering. Leave it all out there on the floor.

I am proud of the risks I've taken on this journey, because living honestly was best for me. That's what we were put on this earth to do.

HEAR'S
THE
THING

((1))

CRANK UP THE VOLUME

Ain't it funny how a melody can bring back the memory.
—CLINT BLACK, "State of Mind"

There was never a day of my childhood that music wasn't blaring in the small house in the suburbs of Columbia, South Carolina, where I grew up. From grade school all the way through middle school, my late father and I listened to the radio through those gigantic Pioneer speakers that took up a third of the living room, hanging onto everything the songs and the DJ had to say between work, school, and dinner. Never a fan of the bass beats constantly hitting the walls and floors, Mom put up with the noise to a point, although occasionally it got to be too much and she'd shout from the kitchen, "Lord have mercy, would you please turn it down!" Five minutes later, we'd turn it back up again.

Few if any words were exchanged between father and son. Occasionally Dad might offer a quick comment of appreciation for a record being spun, but mostly we just cocked our heads in the direction of his old stereo, tuning out the rest of the world so we could take in all that was coming at us over the airwaves.

Dad had an impressive collection of thousands of 45s and albums. The walls of our 1,300-square-foot house were lined with cabinets where he stacked his precious '50s and '60s doo-wop albums, as well as everything from Jerry Lee Lewis to the Big Bopper, along with all the current hits he loved, from artists like Billy Joel, Linda Ronstadt, and Elton John. All day, every day, was like an episode of *American Bandstand*, full of upbeat music. My dad was truly like Dick Clark, knowing exactly what song to play to keep the dance floor full. Or, in this case, the kitchen floor! The look on his face when a particular chord was played, or chorus was sung, said it all. The sounds filled my father with a joy that was infectious, at least to the men in our little household.

"You've been listening to that music since you were the tiniest baby in my womb," my mother would say, only slightly exasperated.

It might not seem like much. It was a lesson that came through gradually, its full significance not quite hitting me until later in life. But in those moments with my dad, I was learning something profound. By being still, silent, and open, I was experiencing the life-changing art of listening. Not only has it been the secret sauce in my career as a country music personality, but it has also been a gift that's strengthened relationships in all areas of my life, from the easy and open dialogue I enjoy with artists and audience members, to my ever-deepening connection with loved ones, friends, colleagues, myself—even God.

Mr. Microphone

Maybe that's what drew me to radio. All those hours just sitting, listening, and developing an appreciation for the art and science of it from the other side. For years, I pretended to be on the radio. It got serious when my parents bought me a Mr. Microphone. Most ten-year-old kids would play with video games, Legos, or maybe GI Joe, but I used to broadcast with Mr. Microphone, tuning into the FM receiver at the low end of the band—around 87.7—and adding my voice to a collection of cassettes with music and shows. Mr. Microphone had a range of about twenty-five feet, so I'd run the wire through a small hole I poked through the screen of my bedroom window, talk from my room, play music, then go to Mom and Dad's car to tune into, well, myself.

As far as I was concerned, this was serious business. If we were sitting at the dinner table past 6:00 p.m., I'd excuse myself to go read the evening news. I scripted whole reports on the weather or the day's events at school and around our neighborhood. I even came up with on-air quizzes with raffles and prizes. First prize was a coupon for dinner at Quincy's Steakhouse, a local restaurant where we went on special occasions. To this ten-year-old, it was like winning the lottery.

Mom and Dad were always a willing audience. Not once did I feel like they were laughing at me. After my broadcasts, they'd comment on my news of the day or say things like, "Oooh, Alan, how can we get one of those prizes?" (My real name is Alan Chavis.) They encouraged me to be me and let my imagination run wild.

The Pirate and the Cherokee

My father, Randy Chavis, and my mother, Jean, could not have seemed more different from each other, though they loved each other fiercely for fifty years until my father passed, and when it came to creating a nurturing environment for me and my baby sister, Missy, they were of one mind. Mom, whose family was descended from Norwegian pirates, looked like the perfect southern belle with flame-red hair and skin as pale and creamy as buttermilk. Dad, who was part Cherokee, was the exact opposite, physically—a handsome teddy bear who liked his southern soul food a little too much for the good of his own health.

It never once occurred to me growing up that my dad, with his dark hair, tan skin, and almond-shaped eyes, would have been slightly outside the bounds of who was deemed acceptable at the time for my mother to date. But Mom couldn't resist him in his military uniform. Dad was on his way to Vietnam until he met her, and just narrowly avoided deployment. Around town they must have attracted some attention, not all of it good, when they first stepped out together at the ages of nineteen and twenty, but they didn't care what other people thought. To hear them tell it, it was a boy meets girl romance worthy of any great country song.

Mom was soft and feminine, never overbearing, but there was an undercurrent of strength. You could tell my mother was the boss and that my father, deferential and loyal, was just fine with the status quo. Both were incredibly loving with each other and us kids. Dad was not one of those men who felt awkward showing affection. It was as if he'd invented the bear hug. That love and reverence was the blueprint for how I would raise my own family one day.

I was blessed to have parents who encouraged and supported me in every hobby, every whim, academic or otherwise. We didn't have much. Mom was the only one with a steady job. She kept the books at a local auto dealership while Dad, who'd suffered complications from diabetes my whole life, cycled in and out of various blue-collar gigs. But I never heard the words, "No, it's too expensive," or "We can't afford it," when it came to anything related to my interests or education.

Soul Food

With all the material challenges they faced, it couldn't have been easy raising a family, but together they managed to create a world for me that felt rich. Both sets of grandparents lived nearby. Every weekend and holiday there were potluck dinners for extended family members or friends, often near the old tobacco farm where my mother's parents lived. Everyone would bring a covered dish with sweet potato pie, butter beans, or mac and cheese. Sometimes we'd have fried chicken with all the trimmings: okra, potato salad, steamed squash, and every casserole imaginable. Other times it was a seafood feast. Many of my uncles were fisherman so, when they hauled a big catch, we'd have fish fries with coleslaw and hush puppies. My nana would also make chicken bog, a traditional dish of Carolina rice slow cooked in a big cast-iron pot, with pieces of chicken stewed for so long the meat fell off the bone. My favorite was my mom's beef pot roast with brown rice, potatoes, and carrots. I'm getting hungry just thinking about it.

My parents were godly folks, particularly my mother, so we went to church almost every Sunday. Outside of that, and regular visits to my father's parents, Grandaddy and Gaga's, house in town, and Mom's folks out in the country, my experiences out-side the home revolved around school. We didn't have the money for exotic family trips other than the occasional road trip to Charleston or Charlotte, North Carolina, or more accu-rately Carowinds amusement park, which was my idea of heaven. Myrtle Beach, South Carolina, and Silver Dollar City in Tennessee (before it became Dollywood) were two other glowing childhood memories of family fun.

My parents and grandparents were determined to give me whatever enriching experiences and exposure to the world they could with what little means they had. They were all about giv-ing me the opportunities they never had. One standout mem-ory was a trip to the 1982 World's Fair in Knoxville, Tennessee, when I was ten. It was a boys' trip that consisted of me, Dad, and my maternal grandfather, Grandpa. Each country was rep-resented with its own tent. I met a Saudi Arabian dressed head to floor in a white robe or dishdasha and had my picture taken with him. Seeing all those nationalities ignited an intense curi-osity about the world. It helped me to imagine myself traveling beyond South Carolina's borders.

School had the same effect on me. In fourth grade, Eastern Airlines had a program that allowed schoolchildren to experi-ence air travel, so my entire class got to take a field trip from Columbia to Charlotte, a twenty-minute trip. It was my first time on a plane, and more material to feed my imagination. The airline crew gave us each a pair of wings and from that moment on I became an avid collector. I never doubted that travel would be in my future, despite my humble, small-town beginnings.

Alex P. Keaton

My parents must have wondered how they ever produced such a driven, ambitious kid. They thought I could do no wrong, which can't have been easy for my baby sister, Missy, who I always felt lived under my shadow.

"You're not like a typical boy, always getting into mischief," Mom told me. "You're my perfect little angel, my gift from God."

I did my chores and kept my room neat as can be, with the bed always made and my toys and clothes put in their proper place. The posters on my bedroom wall could never be dog-eared at the corners. I took measurements and stuck them on straight with double-sided tape. My comic books were stacked neatly in ascending order of the date of issue (I was much more a fan of Batman, in his muscular, formfitting suit, than of Wonder Woman). My Matchbox car collection was ordered according to make and model, each car in its original box.

I was also that nerdy kid who always had my homework done. Think Alex P. Keaton on *Family Ties*. My social life consisted of study buddies, mostly girls, none of them actual girlfriends, although one or two of them may have thought so. In high school I joined the Decca Club and took classes in media and marketing at a nearby vocational school and loved every second of the experience, especially when my teacher convinced me to run for national office. They flew me to Denver where I canvassed for votes, but it worked like the electoral college: the state with the most votes usually wins so a girl from Texas kicked my ass. At least I got to go to Denver, although I didn't see much beyond the airport terminal and the hotel convention center.

That experience must have whet my appetite for politics, because in my junior year of high school, I decided to run for vice president of the student council. The previous year I'd gotten in tight with this crowd, because they were the ones making the decisions about who was going to DJ the school dances, like the Spring Fling or Fall Jam. I'm lucky they chose me most of the time. Yet I was never one of the cool kids. I wasn't an athlete, but I was generally well liked so I figured I had a shot at winning VP. I went all in for my election campaign, making banners with neat, carefully matched lettering. I was all into branding and slogans from my Decca training, and in my teenage brain I believed I'd come up with the perfect one: "Alan Chavis: An Obvious Choice for the Masses." (In retrospect, how obnoxious does that slogan sound?) But I had planned a carefully coordinated guerilla promotional attack on my peers, so they'd get the same message each time they saw my name.

Dressed in my favorite blue blazer and red polka dot tie, which I still have, I delivered a killer speech. Then, timed perfectly with my closing remarks, my banner was the only one among dozens that came unstuck from the wall behind me and fell to the floor. People thought I must have planned it, that I'd arranged for someone below the stage to pull it down with a string. I was mortified. On election day I tried to make up for the signage disaster by asking six of the hottest cheerleaders to turn up half an hour before school started to hold up my banner as the other kids were driving into the school parking lot. They must have liked me enough because they did it. Later that day, in sixth period, during my English class, the school principal announced the winners on the loudspeaker.

I had no idea if I was going to win. I figured that the poster nosedive fiasco the day before must have ruined my chances. Then again, people were whooping and cheering when they saw the girls dance around with my banner in the parking lot. I was sitting at my desk in a state of nervous anticipation, trying not to let my anguish show. It must be how actors and music artists feel when they're nominees at an awards show. The moment they announced my name, "Alan Chavis, Vice President," was the highlight peak of my high school career.

Looking back, I realize I had the popularity edge because I was the kid whose voice was on the airwaves. By the summer before my sophomore year, as soon as I turned fifteen, I got bold and called a local radio station—Yes 97—whose slogan was "It's hard to say no to a station called Yes!" At the time I thought that was brilliant branding. When I called Yes 97, I asked to speak to Leo Windham, the Top 40 morning zoo DJ and owner of the station, whom I'd been listening to as long as I could remember. Amazingly, I got through on the first try and told him I wanted to learn what I could about working in radio. He must have been in a magnanimous mood that day because he said, "Yeah sure, come on by!" From there followed many humble days of hard work. I learned that there are no elevators to success. I knew then, and always assume now, that I will need to take the stairs. After years of practicing exactly what I wanted to do, I wasn't going to accept no, and eventually, I earned my way on air, on a station called "Yes." Finally, my Mr. Microphone obsession had paid off.

Ears Wide Open

All through my childhood, Dad encouraged me in this pursuit because it was also always his dream to be a radio DJ. He never realized his ambition, although he did get to express some of his passion for the music and the mic deejaying an occasional wedding or Christmas party. I watched him as he presented the music, reading the room and knowing exactly what song to play to get people up and dancing or singing along. He never made it about himself when he bantered with the crowd and announced the next record. It was always about the music, but the joy he took in giving his listeners a good time was inspiring.

My father passed that love for music onto me. It was one of the greatest gifts, along with his sense of humor. He was a master of "dad jokes" back before "dad jokes" were cool. If you've ever heard or seen me on air, you know I carry on that legacy as well. Dad also instructed me on the art of the radio patter, naturally and casually making that transition between record spins with interesting factoids about the music or artist. The simple act of sitting and listening to various broadcasts with my father was another early lesson for my radio career. When whatever radio show we were listening to was over, we critiqued the song selections and interviews as if we were program directors. I learned by observing in the safety and comfort of our living room with Dad.

So when I made that call to the local station, I had every confidence I could do this. By then I was just old enough to get my driver's learner's permit in South Carolina. My parents let me borrow their car and off I went. Turns out, the guys at the station were happy to have some free labor, and I fetched coffee for the DJs, organized 4-track carts and CDs, and soaked up everything like a sponge. I stayed humble, keeping out of their way while sticking close by, like an eager little shadow. You don't have to insert yourself into every conversation. In fact, you can often pick up a whole lot more when you just shut up and listen. My big break came when one of the DJs got sick and couldn't work his graveyard shift. Everyone knew I was desperate to get on the airwaves, so the station program director called me and asked if I'd fill in from midnight until 6:00 a.m.

Back then you had to have an FCC license to be on the air, but I had only picked up on that by listening. In anticipation of this moment, I'd already applied. Like a great church Boy Scout, I was prepared! Nowadays, I'm pretty sure that FCC license also means I am fully capable of running a fast-food drive-thru system.

At my age I wasn't allowed to drive after dark, so my mom or dad would selflessly chauffeur me to work in the family car for those late-night shifts. That car was a Toyota Corolla, and she was not cute. A non-sexy, two-door, rust-colored compact with the cloth ceiling hanging down over our heads because all the staples had given up. The Corolla was the kind of car made for practicality and best described as "dependable." But I didn't care. At fifteen, all you want is freedom and some wheels! I soon covered up most of its backside with flair bumper stickers from the station.

I didn't care about the crappy transportation because it got me to my happy place. I loved the feel of that on-air adrenaline radio rush! When I finally went live one summer night in 1988, it was as easy as if I were broadcasting from my bedroom. Except I was taking calls from real people, in real time. I knew more or less what to do when the guys at the station gave me my first shot because, again, I kept my mouth shut and my ears open. These folks didn't even know they were giving me a crash course in broadcasting, because I was there in the background, sweeping the floors and eavesdropping!

All those years of practice and listening to the radio made me a natural. Well, at least no one complained. From that point on they let me fill in whenever I could: weekends, the night shift, anything the other DJs didn't want to do. That's how humbly my illustrious career on the radio began. I still have a trunk full of cassette tapes from all of my broadcasts, collecting dust in my garage. On more than one occasion, I've played an old show of mine on my 1988 Sony boom box and reminisced, remembering why I got into broadcasting in the first place.

My mother still wonders where I got my ambition.

"It was as if you came into this world perfectly formed," she once told me. "All that you do and the way that you are is for a reason."

This thought became a guiding force behind many of the decisions I've made in my life, remembering with every move that I am here for a reason. My mom had a crocheted saying on the wall of our house that read, "You're perfect just the way you are because God don't make no junk!" That one has also always stuck with me.

My parents' way with each other and the rest of the world had plenty to do with how I learned to show compassion. They cared deeply about other people, and it showed in how they listened, paying attention to others in a way that went far beyond polite interest, never making it about them, never really judgy. I was the direct beneficiary of that kind attention. They never imposed their will or ambitions on me. Instead, they showed curiosity about what made me tick, then fed me with constant positive reinforcement, ensuring there were no limits on the life I could see for myself.

I also happened to be a weird kid. Instinctively, I understood the importance of visualizing the life I wanted to lead, then absorbing all I could by listening and paying attention to make it happen. Staying humble enough to hear what others had to say allowed me to take in all the valuable lessons I needed to break into radio, for example, from how to take calls from listeners to how to be prepared when that first on-air opportunity came. Even knowing about the opening at my local station was a result of keeping my ears wide open.

To say I had a vivid imagination would be a huge understatement. I was always living in my head, creating scenes like some kind of mental movie director, writing the dialogue, painting the sets, and, of course, casting myself in the starring role. Listening carefully and absorbing every little detail of information fed those narratives. I could conjure up a whole plot, with a beginning, middle, and an end, visualizing my ideal circumstances, the pithy dialogue, the cast of characters (all my loved ones, friends, and a favorite celebrity, or three).

Stoking the fires of my imagination were the many celebrity gossip and talk shows I never missed. I watched, listened, and soaked up everything I could about the world of entertainment, especially music. This was long before social media and YouTube, where you can get your fill of popular culture on tap. I used to rush home from school just in time to watch Oprah. I *loved* Oprah, the consummate interviewer, who seemed to make every interview not just informative but entertaining. I picked up on the fact that Oprah interviews were more like conversations, and to pull off that kind of show every weekday was a sign of real talent and meticulous preparation.

Then, after dinner, I'd settle on the family sofa to watch *Entertainment Tonight* and, if I didn't have school the next day, *The Tonight Show*. Johnny Carson's way of making his guests the star of his show pulled me in and has been a reference point for my interviewing style ever since. There was a real art to the way he made others shine. I was similarly inspired by the late Larry King, who once said, "I never learned anything when I was talking." Years later, I was blessed to have the opportunity to interview him for CMT.

On weekends I also listened faithfully to Rick Dees's Weekly Top 40 countdown, not just to hear the hottest music but also to hear the smile in Rick's voice. His voice captivated me, plus the show was tight, with snappy jingles ("Rick Dees and the Weekly Top Forteeeeeeeeee!"), and Rick himself always sounded like he was having the time of his life. I imagined myself as Rick and studied his every move. I was beyond thrilled when he launched a late-night TV talk show in 1990. It didn't last long on the air, but I didn't care. He was my hero, and the guy I wanted to be.

A Voice on the Airwaves

In 1989, the year after I landed my first radio job, Dad was diagnosed with a brain tumor, from which he never fully recovered. It caused him to have multiple strokes, and his health declined to the point that he was mostly bedridden in the decade before he passed, in 2017. He was always cheerful, and never one to complain about his condition. Neither did Mom, who dedicated herself to his care until his final days.

Before he left this earth, the highlight of Dad's day was listening to my syndicated shows on the radio. And he counted the days to my weekly appearances on Country Music Television (CMT). Whatever was going on with him healthwise, however much pain he was in, hearing his only son's voice over the airwaves was guaranteed to put a smile on his face. It was the one time of day Mom would let him crank up the volume.

Today, Mom's house is quiet enough to hear the birds chirping outside.

"For fifty years I had to endure your father's music whether I wanted to or not," she told me recently. "But now I really miss it."

This next song's for you, Dad.

• MY BIG BIT OF SUNSHINE •

by Jean, Cody's mom

CODY IS MY GOLDEN SON. Well, I know I'm his mother, and mothers are allowed to say these things, but he really was a remarkable child. I called him my little angel, the apple of my eye, and my big bit of sunshine. He was such a good, gentle-hearted child, as good as could be and not mischievous like typical boys. He never got into fights or came home with black eyes. No, he was different, special, like an old soul. That little boy was God's gift to me, and that's the truth.

He took after his father and me, but mostly me if I'm being honest. The one sure thing he did get from his father was a love of music. Even as the tiniest child he'd have a big pair of earphones on his head whenever he could. But the memory of Cody as he was growing up that stands out most for me was not the way he listened to music. It was the kind way he listened and paid attention to others.

My good friend Phyllis owned a beauty salon near our house. While I was at the salon one day, Cody came by to see me for some reason and he was introduced to Phyllis's mother, who happened to be there. As he was introduced to this little old lady, he shook her hand, covering it with his other hand, then knelt down in front of her chair to chat for a good thirty minutes. They were in their own little world. I'm not sure exactly what they chatted about. Probably some small talk about the weather, how she was feeling that day, and how pretty her new hairdo looked. But he made her feel so special. From then on, Mrs. Carter would ask me about him every time I saw her. Cody was seventeen and she was eighty-five. How often do you see a teenage boy give the time of day to a little old lady?

((**2**))

RAISED ON COUNTRY

So turn it on, turn it up and sing along
This is real, this is your life in a song.
—BRAD PAISLEY, "This Is Country Music"

Country music was the soundtrack to the happiest moments of my childhood: mornings in the kitchen when Mom cooked me a hearty southern breakfast before sending me off to school. While she was frying up some eggs, she'd hum along to Kenny Rogers, Dolly Parton, John Conlee, Conway Twitty . . . whoever was coming through the speaker of our tiny kitchen clock radio, courtesy of our local country music station, "The Great 98," WCOS-FM.

For some, it's smells that bring back a rush of sensory memories. For me, it's sounds *and* smells. Even now, I can't hear "Jolene" without recalling those heavenly scents. The fine fragrance of bacon sizzling in the pan still transports me back to my mother's kitchen. I remember well the sun pouring in through the white lace curtains, making patterns on the oak cupboards and beige Formica countertops (think eighties country chic).

These were the special times, when my baby sister, who is seven years younger than me, was still sleeping in her crib, and I had my mother all to myself. As a parent, we all feel the pressure to put something in our kids' stomachs before they head off to school and, after plenty of negotiation, we're lucky if we can get them to gulp down an Eggo waffle or a Pop-Tart, figuring something is better than nothing. But no one had to cajole this mamma's boy into eating his first meal. I'd usually wake up with a smile, knowing she was fixing me something delicious. She'd get creative too. Fearing I'd get bored, my mom would switch up the eggs and bacon with a grilled cheese sandwich. Some mornings she'd even open a can of Campbell's chicken noodle soup. It just had to be hot—love on a plate—and I'd carry that maternal warmth with me for the rest of the day.

I'd also carry whatever tunes were playing on the radio in my head. You know how a few lines from certain songs tend to stick with you for hours, or days, whether you want them to or not? Well, country lyrics are real sticky. There's nothing like one of these songs to transport you through storytelling, letting your imagination build on the plotlines to take you to all kinds of places.

A great country music song is about real life, plain and simple. Whether it's about love, loss, or just having a good time drinking beer on a Saturday night, there is something in it that pulls an emotion out of you. It resonates with how we live and what we go through. Songs in other formats can do this, but country music does it consistently. There's been some criticism

lately that the production values in a lot of contemporary country songs are almost pop music, and I get that. But the voices
and lyrics are still country, and that's what Nashville does best.
Great songs about real life. This stuff is timeless.

Country music, more than any other kind, taught me *how* to
listen. When I hear a great country song, I pay attention to the
words, and all the emotions behind them. I follow along and
visualize, imagining myself as a bystander in the moment. I'm
completely engaged in the story. I give that same level of focus
to the people I am with. I want to be drawn in, to understand
their whole message.

Country connected with me even as a little kid. The melo-
dies got under my skin, and the lyrics held my attention. It
wasn't just music in the background. I was fully absorbed in the
stories. After listening to these songs over and over again on the
radio, the movie reel in my kid brain would kick in, pondering
the reasons why Jolene couldn't find her own man, picturing
the showdown between Dolly and her love rival, and confused
as to why she'd ever want a man back who cheated on her.

And my childish mind went into overdrive after listening to
"The Devil Went Down to Georgia," by the Charlie Daniels
Band. The devil trying to tempt Johnny to bet his soul in a fid-
dling contest? Johnny accepts the bet and wins a golden fiddle!
Are you kidding me?!

As a small-town kid with loving parents, a doting mother,
and a relatively sheltered home life, maybe I couldn't relate to
all the heartache in some of those songs. The couple that stays
together "Through the Years" (Kenny Rogers), the drifter always remembering the lost love who is "Gentle on My Mind"
(Glen Campbell)—that was heady, grown-up stuff.

Sure, I had my not-so-innocent secrets. Mamma's "little angel" had been slyly subscribing to men's underwear catalogs the

way other boys stockpile old issues of *Playboy* (more on that later). But so many of the great country music songs of my parents' generation dealt with complex emotions far beyond anything I'd experienced. Still, all great art has something for the soul to cling to, and even as a little kid I could relate to that sense of longing when I heard Patsy Cline sing of unrequited love in "Sweet Dreams." That's the beauty of the genre. It speaks to the human condition no matter who we are, or where we happen to be in life.

Cool Again

As I got older, I lost interest in what I considered to be my parents' music. My high school years coincided with the heyday of late '80s pop and rock, so all the cool kids were listening to the likes of Madonna, Prince, and Janet Jackson, and bands like U2, Depeche Mode, Erasure, and Duran Duran. I was a pop culture junkie. Country was nowhere to be heard during these years. As the nerdy kid who desperately wanted to fit in, knowing and playing the most popular music of the day as an aspiring DJ was my entry ticket. Even if I still secretly kinda loved it, as a teenager back then it wasn't cool to admit you were a country music fan. But all that changed when I was eighteen and Garth Brooks exploded onto the scene with "Friends in Low Places," a song that pricked up my ears and started a country music revolution.

It was around that time, right after my senior year of high school, that the radio station where I was working switched its format to country. I thought they were crazy until I started listening to it again. I mean *really* listening. Just like when I was a child listening to the radio with my mother, I was drawn right back into the stories.

Suddenly, there was a new generation of country artists breathing life into the music. Everyone knew the lyrics to Garth's breakthrough hit. He was singing about partying. He was also blowing the top off what the perceptions were about country music, smashing guitars, and running around the stage. He brought show biz to country music, putting on a high-wire act above the audience.

Garth used to talk in interviews about loving the rock group Kiss. He'd also taken notes from the late, great Chris LeDoux, another renegade. Chris had been a bareback rodeo performer who paid tribute to life on the rodeo circuit in his songs and his stage performances, which featured mechanical bulls and fireworks. These guys were bringing back the youth and edge to country and opening the floodgates for a whole new generation of performers.

This happens every so often. There are cycles to country as it keeps getting reinvented by artists, then rediscovered by new generations of fans. As the old Barbara Mandrell song says, many of us were country when country wasn't so cool. Today, it's cool again with the millennial generation, which is going crazy for artists like Sam Hunt and Thomas Rhett, handsome young guys who blend their incredible country voices with a more modern sound. A female artist who represents this new wave is Miranda Lambert, a Texan with her own distinctive, wild edge. These voices, mixed in with traditionalists like Luke Combs and Jon Pardi, are what keep the format vibrant. And today's country wouldn't be the same without Carrie Underwood, whose vocal dominance among all genres is undeniable. Truly, there's a little something for everybody in country music. Luke Bryan may have put it best when he sang, "We're all a little different but we're all the same. Just be proud of what makes you country."

But, in my generation, Garth was the one who got me and so many others hooked. Then I started hearing all kinds of performers in a whole new way. Being open and listening without prejudice can take you to a new level of appreciation. I guess the love of country was always there, but since puberty it had been lying dormant. These guys woke me up. They reignited my passion for country music by making it cool and interesting for kids to love country again.

Garth could write a great party song. But he also had a softer side. Like all great lyricists, he was multidimensional, and could evoke a completely different mood with a ballad like "The River": *Choose to chance the rapids, and dare to dance the tide.* It urges you to dive in and truly live your life to the fullest, despite the risks involved. It relates to my life in many abstract ways I am only just beginning to understand as a grown man.

That's the other thing about a great country music song. It's timeless, and you can grow with it. As you mature and go through your own experiences, you start to hear nuances that you would never have picked up with the innocent ears of childhood. That context gives new depth to the listening experience.

Regular Guy

While I was working in Dallas, I got to meet Garth for the first time. I was doing morning drive radio and still finding my way as a DJ. He was there for a concert and I was invited backstage to meet him before the show. When I walked into his dressing room, he was hunched over the sink, brushing his teeth. I remember thinking, *Man, he's human! This big country rock star is just a regular guy!* That was the first lesson a country artist ever taught me. That they are vulnerable and real, just like us.

Garth was incredibly humble, and gracious. He makes a point of knowing people's names and, even though I was just starting out in my career, he knew exactly who I was.

"Good to see ya, Cody!" he said when he'd finished at the sink. "Have a seat."

We spent a few minutes getting acquainted, then I filled him in on the pre-concert game plan. I was to take a handful of lucky radio listeners to meet him backstage. There were around ten of us, and Garth had spent about half an hour greeting the fans and taking pictures. I watched the way he talked to them, asking them where they were from, who they were here with, and what they did back home. I could tell it wasn't just superficial niceties. Garth was really listening to their answers and fully engaged in the conversation. He was humble enough to understand that everyone is worthy of the time to listen and connect with, because you never know what you'll learn, even or especially from a random stranger.

Soon his road manager came in and told us to wrap it up because another group was waiting to meet the star. Then the manager handed Garth a wad of cash, almost like a roll you'd see somebody pull out at a casino.

"What did y'all spend at the merch stand?" he asked my listeners.

Then he proceeded to go through each one of their bags to reimburse them for the money they'd spent on Garth Brooks T-shirts, hats, and CDs. He personally handed cash over to each one of the fans for everything they had just bought!

"Thank you so much for supporting me," he told them.

That gesture really stuck with me. It was such a cool way to demonstrate how much he appreciated his fans.

I'm sure it can be this way with artists in other genres. If you are lucky enough to get close to them, you will probably see a glimpse of their humble and human side. But from the beginning of my career as a country music DJ, I have found that to be almost always the case whenever I have the privilege of getting to know a country artist. There are no pretensions. What you see is exactly what you get: regular, down-to-earth folks who are disarmingly warm and kind, and who match the personas they project onstage and in their music.

Dolly Parton is exactly the person you see on television. When the cameras aren't rolling, she's still that funny, bright, cheerful woman who has no problem telling you about her wigs and plastic surgery. She may be all fillers and fake eyelashes, but that girlish giggle is real. You don't have to listen that hard to know when someone is sincere. The warmth in her voice and body language was unmistakable. She's still that hicky hillbilly from the hills of Tennessee, and she owns it. Talk about authenticity! But when I met her, I still had to pinch myself. This was the woman I'd been listening to since birth. Being face-to-face with her felt like I was in another dimension. The double "D" dimension!

Condos & Crock-Pots

Taylor Swift is another genuine artist. I first knew her in 2006, when she was just a teenager and I was with a radio station called "The Wolf" in Dallas. This was long before she was the global superstar she is today, but I could see where she was headed. I thought she was the total package: a great singer and songwriter who could perform live, and adorable to boot. She had the goods and yet she was so humble, down-to-earth, and sweet. When I moved from Dallas to Salt Lake City to give my family a full Mormon experience, I was a little nervous about the impact it might have on my career. Sure, there are plenty of country music fans in Utah, but it's not exactly a top-tier market. Then Taylor left me a voicemail I'll never forget:

"Hey, Cody, it's me, Taylor. Congrats! I am so happy and excited for you. I think you are making a move that is awesome for your career and I can't wait to see you at your new station some time."

I was standing in our kitchen when I played that message. It made me feel like it was all going to be okay. More than okay. I had no understanding of what was going to become of either of us, and neither did she, but the fact that she thought well enough of me to make that effort meant a lot.

A few years later, when I was in Nashville at CMT, I had the pleasure of announcing her first nomination for the CMA awards, and letting the world know how proud I was of Taylor. Back then she had a MySpace page, with millions of followers. (Yes, MySpace! It was a thing!) Anyway, she recorded a video of herself watching me make the announcement, and when I said she was among the nominees, she exclaimed: "Codeeee! I am so excited!"

That was a big deal for me. Here was Taylor, already a big country music star, watching *me*. It was one of those heart-stopping 360-degree moments.

Taylor took a lot of flak for being too gushy in her gratitude when accepting her many industry awards. She can be so over the top that people can't believe her excitement is real. But I do, and here's why:

When Taylor first moved out of her mom and dad's house and into a condo in one of the high-rises in downtown Nashville, she told me how she was struggling to get used to living in a place all by herself. She felt weird going back to an empty apartment, and a little spooked by the fact that there were no lights on when she walked in the door. She was barely out of her teens, so it was a big transition, despite her very grown-up career success. So, to make her feel more settled, I bought her a Crock-Pot as a housewarming gift. I figured she could put something on slow cook before she went out, and then come home to the delicious smells when she got home at the end of a day in the recording studio. When Taylor opened the gift box, she went nuts.

"Ohmigosh, ohmigosh, Codeee! I've never had a Crock-Pot before! Thank you so, so much! I love, love, love this!"

Listening well to others has helped me deepen relationships with all kinds of folks. I pick up on things that others might miss, and when I can demonstrate that I was really paying attention with a thoughtful gesture, however small, it means so much to them.

That was the case with Taylor, anyway. You'd think I'd just handed her the keys to a brand-new car or something. It was almost too much. About a week later, Blake Shelton came on my show and mentioned it.

"Man, I heard you on the air giving Taylor Swift, an international superstar, a Crock-Pot. She was so grateful for that Crock-Pot. She loved that Crock-Pot!"

But the enthusiasm was real. That's just who she is: a smiley, bubbly person who gets overwhelmed with gratitude for all the gifts and blessings she's been given. So, if she gets that way about a Crock-Pot, *of course* she's going to go crazy if you give her a Grammy!

On a side note, since Taylor's Crock-Pot, giving slow cookers as housewarming gifts to young country music stars seems to have become my thing. They sort of expect it now. An up-and-coming artist and friend of mine, Kelsea Ballerini, was another recipient. Kelsea was living in my apartment complex for a while, so I introduced her to the joys of Crock-Pot cuisine. She and Taylor also happen to be pals.

I'll keep the Crock-Pot tradition going, but I don't know who will be getting one next. I'll just keep observing and listening until I sense who might need a six-quart slow-cooking oval.

Going Live

By now, you've probably figured out that I am a country music Superfan. And it's not just a love I have for the music. It's the individuals. Each personal encounter I've had with one of these artists has only served to deepen the affection and respect I have for them. More than anything, it's the generosity. You'd think that legends with a string of career accolades would have the odd diva moment. You'd expect someone who gets so many demands for their time and attention might lapse into a jaded attitude. Well, I'm not saying these folks are perfect, but I've never once felt like these stars think of themselves as "stars." No one has tried to put me in my place or keep me at a distance. Instead, they've gone out of their way to support me and lift me up, whether I was a young rookie DJ in local radio, or the TV guy doing the broadcast from backstage at some huge country music festival. They've accepted me as one of their own. Maybe it's just that country music is indeed like family.

Even before I got to know these artists individually, I knew that curating and presenting country music to the world was my vocation. Well before earning my spot on The Wolf in Dallas–Fort Worth, way back when I was working my first full-time radio job at Columbia, South Carolina's WCOS, I became obsessed. "The Great 98," the station I listened to at that carved pine kitchen table with Mom, was like home to me. But, when I was just about to turn twenty-two, they removed me from the 7:00 p.m. to midnight slot at the station and replaced me with a new syndicated show. It was the only time in my career I'd been "fired," although technically I suppose I could have stayed at the station and done a weekend show. Not that it would ever have been enough to satisfy my insatiable ambition. I took it as a sign it was time to move on.

Soon after, I was at a Tim McGraw concert. This was in 1995, after the debut of his third album, *All I Want*, at number one. I was already a fan after hearing his first top country single, "Don't Take the Girl." This guy had it all: good looks, engaging personality, and stage presence. Years later, I wasn't surprised when he launched a successful acting career, because he had a way of connecting with an audience, putting it all out there. But I guess he had to put out a couple of albums before the world really knew who he was. It happens that way sometimes. Success takes hard work and persistence, and even the greatest artists don't always get it right out of the gate. Then Tim started a crossover country explosion with "I Like It, I Love It," and went on to do a major headlining tour. The next day, I wanted to talk on the radio about what I'd seen, to share with my listeners the experience of being in the audience and watching that electric performance. Not being able to do so killed me.

After all, for me, a live country music performance is the whole point. It's everything, because it brings the energy and emotion behind the lyrics directly to the ears of the folks the music was meant for. Any concert or award event where I get to witness an artist do his or her thing with my own eyes is a full-circle moment. I am giving my listeners a dimension of it on my radio and TV show, and even social media these days, but there is no comparison to the full effect onstage where the band plays live, in front of a mic. It's the difference between watching a baseball game on television or going to the ballpark where you can smell the hot dogs and hear the organ playing "Take Me Out to the Ballgame."

It's almost like an escape, where I get to go on an adventure with the lyrics, the music, and the artist. This act of listening is a full-bodied experience. It's about bringing your whole self and all your senses into the moment. You turn off your phone, look up and around you, and soak it all up, feeling the music on a visceral level.

On a smaller scale, I can do this when I am listening to country music in my car, driving on the open road with my windows down. All you do is drive and listen. You're not distracted by other things because you are fully present, letting the music wash over you. And it's that feeling that drives *me*. Whenever I get lost in the "Ryan Seacrest" grind of doing promos, writing scripts, and prepping for interviews, I take myself to a concert to see live music. It always reminds me why I am doing this; why I care about the music so much.

Even though I was a devout Mormon, I have to confess that breathing the same air as my idols and watching them sing in front of me was as much a spiritual experience as any I ever had in a church. So that frustration I felt at not being able to go on the radio the next day and spread the gospel about that Tim McGraw concert motivated me to find a bigger country music radio market. I put together my tapes and resume and scatter-gunned them to every radio station advertising an on-air opening.

Strait Up

It worked. I landed in Orlando, at WWKA, "K-92." This was my big step on my radio career path. At just twenty-two, I'd broken through to a large country music market. That's when I started meeting and interviewing the artists whose music I lived and breathed. Around that time, I'd become a huge fan of the "King of Country Music," George Strait. George was the first mainstream country artist to push back from the crossover pop/country music of the '80s and go "pure" country. But by going back to his roots he had become an innovator. King George evidently felt country had gone too far mainstream. But that didn't mean his retro country style didn't have universal appeal. If someone who knew nothing about the genre were to ask me which artist was most representative, I'd play one of his songs, like "The Chair" or "All My Ex's Live in Texas." The only problem is, I'd have trouble choosing which one. Over the course of his career, he has had sixty number-one hits. That's more number-one songs than any other country artist. With more than one hundred million records sold worldwide, he's one of the bestselling artists of all time, whether in country, pop, rock, or any other category.

But the only way to fully appreciate his greatness is to see him in concert. George designed an "in the round" configuration for his stage, to increase the capacity of the crowds who could see him perform, and he was among the first country artists to do festival-style tours. That dude fully understood the concept of a multilevel listening experience. In fact, he invented it!

On a side note, his June 2014 concert in Arlington, Texas, broke records for the largest indoor concert in North America, with 104,793 people. He's living proof that you don't have to change who you are to have crossover appeal. That's been another big life lesson for me: be authentic, and they will embrace you. King George built it, and they came!

I'd already been to many concerts by the time I met my future wife, Terresa, in Dallas, a little more than a year after my first mind-blowing moment onstage with George in Orlando. She almost had me beat and could recite every single lyric in every single George Strait song word for word. On our second date, I took her to a concert I was covering for KPLX, and it was at that moment I realized I'd found my best friend. I didn't think I'd ever meet a bigger fan than I was. Our throats were raw from singing along, and we were giddy from the thrill of witnessing George live onstage. There's an energy to these concerts. You don't just watch passively. You are actively participating in the experience. And finding someone who shared my passion doubled the joy.

After the concert, I took Terresa backstage. George greeted me like an old friend, then turned his attention to the petite blonde beauty who was standing beside me.

"Hey, what's your name?" he asked her.

Terresa went blank for a minute.

She turned to me and asked, "What's my name?"

I couldn't help but laugh, as did George.

Then, before I could answer, she turned back to George and said, "I know you're George Strait and I'm, I'm . . . Terresa." She broke into an embarrassed grin.

She was so excited, and nervous, to meet her longtime music idol that she momentarily forgot her own name! George couldn't have been more gracious. I probably should have popped the question that night, because there is no way she would have said no.

The Ice Bath

I met a bunch of my idols while working in Texas. My time at The Wolf brought me into contact with the biggest names in country music, often from the earliest stages of their careers. They knew the station as a powerful influencer on the country music market and loved the fact that we didn't just rely on some chart list out of Nashville. We had our ears to the ground, and we really listened for talent, whether it was some kid with star potential selling out in the honky-tonks of Fort Worth, or artists already at the top of their game, enjoying the full support of a record label. We didn't care where a great country record came from. It just had to be authentic.

Maybe that's why I became good friends with Dierks Bentley. He was still a newbie to the country music scene, but he wanted to be pals early on. After our first conversation, he gave me his number and told me to text him anytime. Dierks was just a regular, easygoing guy, and we hit it off on a purely human level.

"I love that you're willing to take chances on new artists," he once told me.

Dierks understood my genuine passion for the music, and the fact that we could have deep conversations about the meaning of the songs we both loved so much. He was a fellow listener who always loved a deep dive into great lyrics.

When I first got the job at CMT several years later, I requested Dierks for my first interview. I knew he'd show up for me, and that he'd do everything he could to make me feel comfortable for my big Nashville debut.

Well, maybe he doesn't *always* try to make me feel comfortable. Dierks likes to take ice baths. It started with his annual polar bear lake jump on New Year's Day and has since morphed into an extreme pre-performance ritual he takes with him on the road. At every tour stop, he fills a sixty-five-gallon garbage can with ice and water, strips down to his skivvies, and jumps in. He stays in there for a minimum of twenty minutes, taking deep meditative breaths to withstand the frigid water.

Dierks was inspired by the Wim Hof method, named after the Dutch daredevil who has trained himself to stay submerged in frozen waters for as long as two hours! Known as the "Iceman," Wim Hof claims health benefits like a boost to the immune system, better sleep, and an endorphin rush.

"It's something I try to do daily, actually," Dierks told me. "This is where I get all my energy for the show. You come in here, you do this for twenty minutes, and you walk out onstage ready to rock."

He recently invited me to join him in one of these ice baths when we were backstage in Cincinnati on his "What the Hell" tour. I could hardly say no, but I sure as heck didn't relish the idea. Growing up, I never was the guy who enjoyed strutting around by the pool with my shirt off. I was always the pipsqueak in gym class who felt slightly inferior and struggled with body image. But years later, after discovering a passion for fitness and lifting weights regularly, I finally had a body I was proud of. So there I was, about to take the frigid leap, shedding some vulnerabilities while the cameras were rolling.

This had been a year of pushing myself well past my comfort zone, and Dierks knew it. There was almost a twinkle in his eye when he threw down the challenge. So, I gamely took off my clothes and stepped into a pair of swimming trunks while they prepared a "bath" that looked more like a giant slushy, only much less inviting.

"We have EMTs standing by, because you never know," Dierks said. He was dead serious.

How reassuring, I thought. Then, appropriately, I understood better why Dierks named his tour "What the Hell."

There was a quick photo op. Dierks and I were standing behind the buckets, and his manager asked us to stand beside them because you could only see us from the waist up and we looked, well, naked.

"People might get the wrong idea after my recent big news," I quipped, wisecracking in a way I never would have dared before I'd come out of the closet. Everyone laughed, especially Dierks.

"Okay now, on the count of three," Dierks said. "One, two, three!"

I took a deep breath and plunged myself into a giant bucket of ice cubes, only to shriek, "Holy shit, that's cold!" and leap out nanoseconds later. I tried again, this time a little more mentally prepared.

"You've got to breathe your way through it," Dierks coaxed. "Don't fight it. Invite it."

I took his advice. I breathed through it. Well, more like gasped at first. Then I focused on the here and now, listening to the voice in my head that said *you can do this*, and pushed through the pain. By minute seven, it felt like my skin was going to melt off. I'm pretty sure my nipples had frozen off at that point. But then I went into the zone and made it all the way to minute thirteen, which I was told was impressive for a first timer. By the time I slipped out of that bucket, wrapped myself in a towel, and slowed down the violent shivering, I felt exhilarated. The experience made me realize that I don't have to be afraid. I can do anything. It's not so much that I am invincible, but I can endure. I can come out the other side stronger, wiser, better.

Being a lifelong listener of country music has taught me that much. Or I should say, the country artists themselves were my teachers. I've been blessed to be surrounded by so many talented, compassionate, and inspiring folks over the years. It seems like members of the Nashville community have been there at all the major inflection points of my life, urging me on with their lyrics, their examples, their kind gestures and words to propel me on my personal and professional path. These are my people. This is where I belong.

Earlier, I talked about the spiritual experience of attending a concert or cranking up the car stereo with the windows rolled down. It's exactly like the Maren Morris song "My Church" says:

When I play the highway FM / I find my soul revival . . .

And the artists and fans are my congregation. That's one of many reasons why the 2017 shooting at the Route 91 Harvest music festival in Las Vegas, killing 58 and injuring 869, hurt so much. It was such a violation.

In the past, I had covered the event for CMT, but not that year. I would have been standing right up front and in the cross-hairs when that shooter opened fire. I could picture myself as a part of that crowd. These were the faces of the country music fans I see every day. Nashville is still in mourning, because these were our fans, our family.

As I went through the names on my radio and television shows, talking about each individual who had passed, it hit me hard. There were boyfriends and girlfriends on first dates, gay couples, young men drinking beer, husbands and wives cele-brating their anniversaries. This broad cross section of people—"All Kinds of Kinds" as Miranda Lambert sings—is what country music, and America, is all about: folks who are different but still belong, like me. In fact, two of the largest mass shootings in our country's history have involved my two most beloved tribes: country fans in Vegas and members of the LGBTQ+ community at the Pulse nightclub in Orlando a year earlier.

Since the Vegas tragedy, I have interviewed several of these survivors individually, and each time it has reinforced something I've kind of always known: listening can be one of the greatest acts of compassion. You shut up and let them speak. You simply let them tell the story of their loved one who has passed, interjecting just enough to let them know you understand.

Their actions also showed that, in the face of evil, there is an overwhelming amount of good in the world. Country fans rose up and risked gunfire to help each other on that tragic night. And, despite the gun-toting stereotypes, many spoke up afterwards about ways to make the world a safer place. Vegas, and what happened in the aftermath, demonstrates how the country music family is continually evolving to become more inclusive, hearing each other and hopefully becoming more compassionate.

These are my people, and I love them with all my heart.

(((3)))

MORMON ON A MISSION

Taking a chance I might
Find what I'm looking for.
—SUGARLAND, "Something More"

My first big crush was a Mormon. He was a ripped soccer player with sandy blond hair and piercing blue eyes. He had sculpted broad shoulders and the most muscular legs I'd ever seen on a high school senior. In other words, he was everything I was not, including super straight. He became my best friend one summer, and he had no idea.

To get closer to this guy, I started attending his church. Then something shocking happened. I listened with an open heart and mind to the sermons and fell in love with the message. There was just something about Mormonism that spoke to me. I guess it found me right at a moment in my life when

I was searching for something. My raging teenage hormones needed to be channeled, regimented, into holier pursuits, or so I believed.

When I told my parents that these visits to the Mormon church were something more, and that I'd decided to join the church, they were beside themselves. Mom especially. She has always been a deeply spiritual woman who is firm in her faith. One day, when I was about seven years old, we were driving somewhere when she pointed to a violet sky flecked with pink-tinted clouds from a setting sun and described the rapture, or at least what she imagined the rapture would look like from all her Bible reading.

"Just imagine, the kingdom of heaven right up there where we can see it, with trumpets playing and our Lord and Savior Jesus Christ appearing in the air!"

Mom went on to describe how we, and all other believers, dead or alive, would ascend to Christ. All our loved ones who'd passed, all our ancestors, would receive their resurrected bodies. We'd all be made perfect in the eyes of our Lord, and up we'd float. Then Mom went on to quote the scriptures, as she often did:

> For the Lord himself shall descend from heaven with a shout, with the voice of the archangel, and with the trump of God: and the dead in Christ shall rise first: Then we which are alive and remain shall be caught up together with them in the clouds, to meet the Lord in the air: and so shall we ever be with the Lord. Wherefore comfort one another with these words.
>
> —1 Thessalonians 4:16–18

I saw what she saw. I felt what she felt, as if my body were already floating skywards. An imaginative kid who'd inherited his faith, and then some, from his mother, these images seemed as real as the cracked piece of country road we were driving along.

"I can't wait until the rapture is here!" I told my mother. "I can't wait for that day."

Roadside Prayer

As a deeply spiritual kid from the time I can remember, it wasn't all that hard for me to believe in miracles. And prayer was as natural to me as breathing. Like the time when I was a couple of years older and Mom and I found ourselves by the side of the highway waiting out a violent storm. We were on our way to my grandparents' house about a hundred miles from our house via the I-20. What felt like hurricane-force winds rattled our little car, and hail stones the size of golf balls fell on its roof and hood with such velocity we thought for sure we were either going to get crushed or blown away into the empty tobacco fields nearby. We felt vulnerable and exposed to the wrath of Mother Nature. Mom couldn't hide her panic.

"Oh, what are we going to do?"

"Pray," I told her, then we both sat and did just that. Seconds later, the winds died down and the hail bombings stopped. Our prayers were answered, and we went on our way.

In a way, although Mom would probably hate to hear it, she laid the foundation for me to accept many of the tenets of the Mormon faith. She was always telling me about the Second Coming and what it might be like in heaven, and her stories captivated me. Mormonism linked up well with what I already felt. It didn't seem all that different to what I'd been taught. To me the angels were real, and the story of Jesus was true. So why couldn't Joseph Smith have discovered another volume of scripture delivered by an angel? It all seemed perfectly reasonable.

Most non-Mormons dismiss the religion as a little odd, and I get it. Polygamy, long underwear or "temple garments," and no coffee, much less alcohol. My mother, a Southern Baptist girl, was as confused as she was disappointed when I told her I wanted to become Mormon. We attended several different Christian churches growing up from Nazarene to Baptist, but they were all in that southern tradition of the faith, so when I veered onto a different path there was a sense of shock and betrayal from her and some in my family.

Under My Skin

I couldn't help being drawn to the faith. My heart spoke loud and clear. There was a kindness and compassion to the Mormon doctrine that got under my skin in a way that those other churches did not. Mormons have a strong sense of community and dedicate their lives to serving others. They are family oriented and committed to doing the right thing, always. And the music of those soaring voices of the Mormon Tabernacle Choir gave me chills. It reached me at a visceral level, distracting me almost completely from the perfectly formed male standing next to me at church, in his crisp white shirt and tight black pants. I could actually *feel* the Holy Ghost in the church's music. For a kid desperately searching for something that would help him transcend his inner turmoil and be a part of something bigger than himself, the timing of my exposure to that faith could not have been better.

I always had a strong impulse to connect with other people. I was eager to please and be liked, but it was much more than that. Mom called me her "ball of sunshine" because I had this need to make other people smile, even from the time I could crawl. It didn't matter who they were, or where they were from. I was curious about any stranger I met, and if someone in a room looked uncomfortable, I'd lock in on them, draw them out with questions, and listen carefully to what they had to say to find out what I could do to fix it. Maybe I was a born entertainer, because being able to have a positive impact on someone else's state of mind felt like such a blessing. Or maybe I was also a frustrated therapist. Either way, building those connections made the hairs on the back of my neck stand up, like a spiritual rush.

Cross Country

Mormonism gave me a chance to use that impulse in a structured way, with a clear sense of purpose, almost like the military. So, when a friend from church approached me and said I should go on a two-year mission in Seattle, I couldn't pass up the chance. That's probably what broke Mom's heart more than anything. It seemed like no one ever considered moving beyond the zip code, and here I was, at eighteen years old, planning to live clear across the country, 2,828 miles from everyone I'd ever known and loved.

There were plenty of tears when I made the announcement in our family living room, mostly from Mom, who had to watch her firstborn dive headlong into what seemed to her a radical religion. Dad was more bewildered than anything. As a parent now, I can't imagine having to say goodbye to my son, Landon, for two years, with nothing but intermittent phone calls to keep me connected.

Yet, somehow, they found the strength to love me through it, embracing a decision they disagreed with because it was mine to make. Soon after I'd joined the Mormons, my parents made the effort to attend some of the services and get to know a few of the families. We were invited to dinners at the homes of some of the folks who were part of the church in the area and, to her credit, Mom didn't miss a single opportunity to mix it up with some Mormons. She had plenty of motive.

"If my son is gonna leave our church and be a part of this new community, I'm going to make it my business to understand what it's all about," Mom said.

Grandpa sweetly and politely asked me about my newly adopted religion. His brother had married a Mormon woman and moved away to Pocatello, Idaho, so he already had some sense of what I was getting myself into and knew the questions to ask. We had long, deep conversations about the faith because he sincerely wanted to understand what his brother and I believed, and why. It gave Mom some comfort to know that I would be going to her uncle's house in Idaho for a few days before being taken to the Mission Training Center in Provo, Utah. Maybe, she thought, since another family member believed, Mormonism wasn't so wacky after all.

On the day of my departure, Mom, Dad, Grandpa, and a few friends saw me off at Columbia's local airport. It was only ten minutes from our house, which was right on the flight path. It was tense on the ride over. Mom chitchatted about my immediate plans when I got there, whether I had remembered to pack enough socks, and the lunch she'd packed for my long journey across the country. But it was all she could do to stop her voice from trembling as she fought back the tears.

I felt elated. Here I was, embarking on a brand-new adventure that no one else in my family but me would get to experience. It was another example of taking the road less traveled. I believed I was doing something noble with this new tribe that was all mine, so I could hardly contain my excitement. But I was also being selfish. At eighteen, I didn't have the wisdom to understand how hard it must be to watch a child head for the farthest point in the continental United States, a place that would be my home for the next few years. It's not as if my parents could afford the plane tickets to come visit. They'd have to content themselves with the occasional phone call or a letter. Even a new military recruit gets more home leave and access to family. But as they saw me off to the departure gate, which you could do in those days, I scarcely gave them a backward glance.

When Great Uncle Billy picked me up from the airport at Salt Lake City, I was struck by how similar he looked to my grandfather, his brother. With the same bald head and square, wire-rimmed glasses, they could have been twins. While he looked familiar, the rugged landscape appeared new, strange, and mesmerizing. Pocatello was just a whistle stop from Yellowstone Park to the north, and about a two-hour drive along the interstate to Salt Lake City, with rolling hills and mountains. It was a huge contrast to the terrain of South Carolina's Midlands and Low Country, with its swamps, lakes, and oak trees full of hanging moss. I rested with my relatives for a few days and adjusted to the thin mountain air before they drove me to the training center, a kind of boot camp for Mormon missionaries.

I loved the experience. It was a total immersion into the Mormon way of life and belief system, and I was pumped to get started converting people and saving souls in Seattle. The rules and expectations were clear. I was to go door-to-door in my designated area, the Book of Mormon tucked under my arm. The training session covered everything about how to greet strangers when they open the door. We'd start with a few introductory questions.

"Have you ever heard of the Book of Mormon?"

"Would you like to live forever, together with your family?"

"Do you want a closer relationship with Jesus Christ?"

The idea was to start out gently, engage the audience, get them curious about Mormonism. If we somehow managed not to get a door slammed in our faces, our goal was to entice with kindness and empathy. Politeness was key. And listening. The best way to get someone to listen to you is to listen to them first.

I embraced this approach wholeheartedly. It felt natural to a boy as gregarious as I was. Added to my natural skills was the church training, which taught me ways to disarm people even in the tensest of situations. The soft approach involved being passive, asking questions, and finding common ground to let a perfect stranger into my story. I've used what the Mormons call "teaching by gentle persuasion" throughout my career in radio and television, with the management teams at radio stations, even with my team today. It's about making others feel comfortable.

It wasn't about preaching, necessarily. I wasn't there to prescribe what others should do. Instead, if I was lucky enough to get them to open the door a few more inches, I'd dig deep and say what I would do, or how Mormonism had helped me personally, extending a solution to them that's helped me in my life. It was tricky, because I had to try not to make these conversations about myself, yet these conversations about spirituality needed to be personal. It was a way of humbly describing those moments when I've needed guidance.

These conversations tested me. More than once, I was challenged to defend my faith. It forced me to dig deep and ask myself, *Do I believe this and, if I do, if I even want to believe it, how do I help someone else believe what I believe?*

Uphill Battle

My first week in Seattle was rough. On a Mormon mission you do everything in pairs, to keep an eye on each other, and my "companion" and I had been assigned an area that was especially hilly. We had to navigate our way around on bicycle, huffing, puffing, and sweating our way up the streets in our snug-fitting dress pants, shirt, and tie. But it was the loneliness that got me. It also happened to be Christmas week when it finally hit me how much I missed my family. The people I was with in the field did their best to make me feel better, but they were virtual strangers to me and I really felt the miles between me, Mom, Dad, my sister, my grandparents, and everyone in South Carolina. On Christmas Day, a family from the local Mormon church hosted us, feeding us turkey, stuffing, and all the fixings. *It's a Wonderful Life* was playing in the back room on the television, but while we were on mission, we weren't allowed access to TV or radio.

"Go ahead, watch it," the family patriarch told us. "It's Christmas. We won't tell!"

It gave me so much comfort. And perhaps for the first time, I grasped the full meaning of the classic movie. Jimmy Stewart's character, George Bailey, is taught through his trials the important difference one life can make and the ripple effect of how just one action impacts so many people. That idea sunk in deep that evening and made the next day a little better.

But over the next few weeks I came so close to walking away from it all. As a recent convert, I was permitted to write home.

I was even allowed the occasional call to my parents, a luxury most missionaries didn't get so regularly. The love and acceptance in their voices, and the assurance that they would always be there for me when and if I decided to come home, helped me get through the next day, and the next. I knew I'd have to be all in every day for the next two years.

It was a monk-like existence. I lived in barebones living quarters with a bunch of other young men, getting up at dawn to pray, eat breakfast, and make my bed before spending the day knocking on the doors of strangers spreading the gospel according to Joseph Smith. You become so focused on the higher purpose that you check your ego, your sense of individuality, at the door. The rules were so strict, I couldn't even listen to my beloved country music, just MoTab (that's what hip Mormons call the Mormon Tabernacle Choir). That being said, when I wasn't jamming to the choir, I would occasionally sneak out with my Walkman and listen to some contraband cassettes and local radio stations, tuning in to country DJ Tony Thomas on the legendary call letters KMPS. And I probably used the house phone (this was before cell phones) to reach out to kindred spirits more than I should have, sneaking into the hallway to make calls while my companion was sleeping or in the shower.

Besides the homesickness, I had some serious doubts about certain aspects of the Church of Jesus Christ of Latter-day Saints. For starters, the fact that black people weren't allowed to reach priesthood until 1978 concerned me deeply. The Mormon Church has a strict hierarchy, and the fact that they excluded a population from the highest echelons for so long stuck in my craw.

Then there was the obvious issue of Mormonism's rejection of homosexuality. Although I was always trying to push it aside, I knew I was gay, although I never acted upon it, although some of the good-looking missionaries around me certainly caught my eye. I was always trying to be what I thought God wanted me to be. I was conscientious and determined to play by the rules, and if that meant somehow casting aside my internal wiring, I was willing to do that to be part of this thing that I believed was much bigger than myself. The church had a way of saturating my life, to the point where I put the things that troubled me into a locked box, deep in the recesses of my mind. But every now and then those doubts would creep up to the surface.

Polygamy was another bugaboo of mine. Although the practice had long since been banned by the official Mormon Church, it still went on under the radar, in offshoot congregations. And it was hard to forget that Brigham Young, the founder of Salt Lake City and the second president of the church, had fifty-five wives! Joseph Smith himself is said to have had up to forty wives, some underage. Polygamy was and is held up as one of the "rewards" in heaven, if not on earth. Mormons believe in producing spirits by bringing children into the world, which only happens through reproduction. While I always wanted kids and imagined the family in the little house with the white picket fence, akin to the way I was brought up, as a gay man the idea of sister wives horrified me. It was bad enough that I had to figure out a way to be with one woman.

Guiding Voices

When I finally hit that crossroads, plagued with doubts and tough living conditions, I reached out to my mission head, President McFarlane, who was always kind and wise. He immediately came to the shabby residence I shared with my mission companion and sat with me on one of the threadbare reclining chairs, listening intently as I shared some of my doubts and fears.

"I don't think I can do this anymore, President McFarlane," I told him. "I'm so sorry I failed you and the Lord, but I believe it's time for me to go home."

Shockingly, he told me, "If you want to go home, I support you 100 percent."

What? I thought, expecting more resistance to my wishes.

"I would like you to stay, but I will love you and respect your decision, no matter what."

Those words stayed with me. I always had this fear that if I sinned or failed someone, I would not be loved. I'd be rejected by my community, by God. But the opposite was true. This sweet, fatherly man made me feel unconditionally supported. When I finally did decide to stay, it wasn't out of a fear of disappointing others. I didn't feel coerced, guilty, or resentful. It was made in the fullness of my heart, and I felt so much better about it as a result. President McFarlane's approach is one I've emulated time after time as a father. Whenever one of my kids came to me with a problem or a difficult decision they had to make, I just listened without judgment, and told them they'd be loved 100 percent whatever they chose to do.

I encountered a lot of church members like my mission president. They made it easier for me to stay. When we weren't knocking on doors, we were being cared for by members of the congregation. Families would have us over for meals on Sundays, serving us glasses of milk (because we weren't allowed to drink much else) with generous helpings of meat loaf, lasagna, pizza, and casseroles. We played basketball and board games together. We formed real friendships.

That sense of community was powerful. It made it easier for me to look past some of the flaws of Mormonism. Like any human, the church was far from perfect, but there was so much good. I went with that feeling, sharing my thought process with people I was trying to convert who had similar misgivings. Acknowledging the imperfections of the church and being open about my own struggle proved to be far more effective than glossing over the truth. My sincerity at least won me their trust and kept my foot in the door long enough to be heard.

Two of my dearest friends from the Seattle congregation were Wayne Quinton and his wife, Jeanne. Wayne was an extremely successful entrepreneur from the Seattle area who'd invented the treadmill used in hospitals for EKGs and was instrumental in inventing the catheter. This older couple, who lived in a private neighborhood in the Highlands full of Mc-Mansions, were mega rich. Yet they were incredibly humble.

Wayne and Jeanne often had me over for meals. They treated me as if I were their son, as their own son was serving a mission in Japan at the same time I was serving in Seattle. For a lost nineteen-year-old with so many doubts, their presence in my life was reassuring, like a second set of parents. They were instrumental in helping me work through some of my thorniest questions about the faith, patiently talking things through with me, helping me with my "testimony," which in Mormonism is a statement of your beliefs in front of other members of the congregation, inspired by the Holy Ghost. Typically, you prepare for this initiation into the faith through lots of reading, quiet contemplation, and deep conversation with God. When that knowing comes, you recognize it with a sense of peace, a feeling of elation, a burning in your heart, or a voice in your head. I experienced all of the above.

But my friendship with the Quintons wasn't just based on heavy conversations about Mormon theology. We had a true kinship. On one occasion, Jeanne asked me what my favorite dish from home was, so she could try her hand at cooking it for me. I attempted to describe the brown Carolina rice my mother used to make with pot roast. I didn't know exactly how Mom cooked it, but I've since learned the recipe: brown rice, French onion soup, beef consommé, and about a pound of butter. I could eat this fluffy, delicate grain any time of day, as a side dish or a meal. Bless her heart, Jeanne did her best, but the end result tasted pretty awful. I smiled and chewed my way through it, but no matter the taste, the heart in Jeanne's attempt meant everything.

Wayne often joined me on our Wednesday night visits to the home of Charlotte Jones, an older lady on my mission route who loved the attention of all the missionaries who came knocking. She was a jovial lady full of chitchat and smiles. Our goal was to figure her out so that we could convince her to get baptized into the church, but no one ever did until Wayne and I worked our charm to convince her. She was among my first baptisms in Seattle. It was exhilarating knowing I'd helped someone make that profound spiritual decision.

After her baptism, Charlotte came to church in the boldest colored dresses I'd ever seen, often with flowery scarves and a pearl necklace. She seemed to truly relish her newfound faith, and everyone in the congregation loved her right back.

Door-to-Door

Meanwhile, for all the small triumphs, there were countless failures and hours spent trying to save souls, with polite nods at best, and doors slammed in our faces at worst. Some of my fellow missionaries even had objects thrown at them in the streets. We did most of our "tracting," which is the Mormon term for knocking on the doors of potential converts, in the poorest, roughest neighborhoods of Seattle. We figured the tougher the circumstance and the more humble the existence, the more need people may have for answers. On one strip of run-down houses, the neighbors suggested we try our luck with a guy named James, who'd just been released from jail for drug use.

When we came to his place, we knocked gently and the door swung open. The place looked like a crack den. James, a hulking guy with a ponytail, piercings, and covered in tattoos all the way up to his neck, stood at his threshold, looming over us as we stood on the doorstep below.

"Um, uh, hello, er, I'm Elder Chavis and this is Elder Johnson," I stammered, praying I would not get punched in the face. "We're from the Church of Jesus Christ of Latter-day Saints, and we have a message for people in the neighborhood."

"Well, come on in!" James said, suddenly beaming (and possibly relieved we were not parole officers).

Oh crap, I thought, momentarily wondering if this was a trap. *Any witnesses around?* I wondered, looking over my shoulder before stepping inside. But he turned out to be a sweetheart who'd been trying to figure himself out and was thirsting for spiritual guidance. It wasn't long before he joined the church. Last I heard, he was slipping back to his old ways and smoking weed, but it was a victory while it lasted.

Also among my journeys in Seattle, I won over Mike Boonsripisal, the son of immigrants from Thailand. He was just seventeen when we first knocked on his door. We introduced ourselves and he immediately invited us in. He had friends at school who happened to be Mormons and Mike wanted to learn more. Over the next few months, we chatted a lot. Mike loved having us over. Finally, we asked Mike if he'd like to be baptized. For him, it was a no-brainer, but he needed permission from his parents who were Buddhists. They had some misgivings. Mormonism was completely foreign to their Thai customs. Knowing how that felt from my own experience, I could give Mike additional support on his conversion journey and share my optimism that his folks would eventually come around.

We prayed about Mike's baptism in church and in our morning and nightly missionary prayers. One day, my companion and I "blessed" Mike by placing our hands on his head to ask God for all His support for Mike and his family. Eventually, Mike's parents did consent and today Mike is a successful member of the church, with a wife and family of his own.

Another win was Mark Papritz, who was dating a Mormon girl. Before their relationship could go much further, his girlfriend asked him to learn about her faith. But Mark had the same questions I had. Polygamy and bigotry were not great selling points. Over the span of months, we had long conversations as Mark challenged and I attempted to defend my faith. Finally, I acknowledged to him that I had the same doubts and shared how I dealt with it. Being human, saying, "Yeah, I don't get that part either," was what finally won him over. It let him know he was not alone in his questioning. If I struggled yet could get past those doubts and still love aspects of the Mormon Church, maybe he could too. Eventually Mark got baptized. It was probably my greatest success story on my mission.

During those two years in Seattle, I attempted to find myself, and this Mormon adventure was all-consuming. When you join the church, it's not just something you do on Sundays. It's 24/7. Everyone has jobs, and what Mormons term "callings," whether they are teaching Sunday school to young kids or gospel to the congregation. There was always something to keep you busy.

I brought a lot of the lessons I learned on my mission with me throughout the rest of my life, although I am not the same guy I was then. Over the decades, my faith has evolved with wisdom, experience, and self-acceptance. It took me a long time to realize that institutionalized religion, despite its many virtues, does not have all the answers, and that even the most extreme measures cannot change who you are. I will admit I am still in that process of discovery.

Possibly the greatest gift Mormonism gave me was the space and discipline to be still in moments of prayer and silence, so that I could listen to my intuition and God's voice. I also developed the ability to build a rapport and trust with complete strangers even in the most unlikely of circumstances. I learned to set aside my assumptions about the people who lived on the other side of the door. I didn't know what they were going through, or even whether they were believers. Before I could even think about getting across their threshold, much less try to convey my message and spread the Mormon gospel, I had to show curiosity, care, and concern about their lives by asking thoughtful, probing questions. And I had to follow up with comments and clarifications that demonstrated I could catch every nuance of what they were feeling and where they were coming from.

I don't regret that time in Seattle. I met wonderful people and felt a deep sense of partnership with other young men who shared the same mission: helping others. I wanted to be the best possible human I could be and live as close to what I felt righteousness looked like. I was probably also trying to fill a void. Nothing sexual—gay or straight—happened. No way was I going to go there. By the time I ended my mission, I was still a virgin. Instead, I was channeling all my energies into a higher purpose and serving God in the hope that He would somehow "cure" me down the road. Little did I know that was never His plan for me.

(((4)))

THE WOLF

The road goes on forever and the party never ends.
—ROBERT EARL KEEN, "The Road Goes On Forever"

Miranda Lambert is a crafty little thing.
Let me explain.

As radio DJs, we have the power to influence listeners and give new artists their first big chance to be heard outside of the honky-tonks and clubs where they play. And never more so than at KPLX-FM, The Wolf, in Dallas, a radio station that dominated the airwaves of the biggest country music market in America. We were rebels: true industry disrupters. We prided ourselves on our ability to pick out an artist or a song that our Texan listeners would love. We weren't interested in what the record labels were trying to sell, unless we believed it was genuinely great. Just because a record was on the Top 10 in

Nashville didn't mean we'd give them a spin on our station. We played mainstream Nashville country, of course. But Texas is a whole different music scene, and we were loyal to our local artists.

I was the music director, a role I relished. We were always on the lookout for new artists and songs and, apparently, I had a knack for spotting the next big star. It was a question of scavenging through all the demo tapes sent our way. I loved that hunt. As a pure fan who paid close attention to the blend of lyrics and music, I prided myself on knowing a hit when I heard one. I guess that's why I won Music Director of the Year nine times during my ten-year tenure at the station.

In 1997, when I first got to the Dallas–Fort Worth area, one of the best sources for talent were the Texas honky-tonks. When I saw lines of people going around the block, I got curious about who the artist was and stopped by for a listen. They were almost always Texans like Jack Ingram, Pat Green, or Robert Earl Keen. A Nashville artist could never fill those bars up with fans the way a Texan country artist could, and we gained a huge following because we were brave enough to deploy these artists into the mainstream. And if we played a song, everyone's head would turn in Nashville. That's how much influence we carried.

The more we listened to what was out there at the grassroots level, the better we got at picking up on things that everyone else missed. No one in our industry was noticing the fact that our homegrown Texan talent was killing it. They were so laser-focused on what was coming out of Nashville that they were deaf to the pure gold that was right there on the doorstep.

I am proud to say I "discovered" a few new artists while at The Wolf, but I can't take credit for Miranda. Just a teenager at the time, she was already making her own music and singing her own songs, although she hadn't yet broken through. She caught our attention when she delivered these homemade cowboy hats along with her demos to our door. They were awesome: painted red, white, and blue like the Texas flag and bedazzled with beer bottle caps around the edges. It was an ingenious marketing move. Or I should say, crafty. For a gorgeous hat like that I just *had* to listen, and I was blown away. We started playing her music regularly, and before long she was on *Nashville Star*, a country music reality TV singing competition. Shortly after, she got her first big record deal.

I sure wish I still had that hat!

Wet Behind the Ears

Of course, The Wolf didn't exist as we know it when I first got there. By the late '90s it was still called "K-Plex," the third-most-listened-to country music station out of three in the Dallas market, an also-ran that was straining for relevance with a bunch of older jocks stuck in their ways, uninterested in rising country musicians or what their listeners might actually be into hearing. And when I showed up, a young fella at twenty-three, fresh from a second-tier radio market in Orlando, it wasn't exactly a warm reception.

It's not that I was totally without experience. After my Mormon mission, I worked for my local radio station back home in Columbia. In my spare time I studied communications in college for a couple of semesters, but it wasn't enough. I was burning with ambition and, much as I loved being back home and eating Mom's cooking, I felt stuck. Then, in 1995, I leapfrogged to the number one country music station in Orlando, K92.3. When the opportunity came along, I figured I could make it in radio without that college degree and, as always, my parents supported me in my decision even though I wasn't following a straight line. My dad, who was already bursting with pride that he got to listen to his son's voice on his local station, was thrilled for me.

Fortunately, the program director in Orlando, Mike Moore, saw something in me.

"You're way better than the market you're in," he told me over the phone. "If you're willing to come down here and do a show, K-92 would love to have you!"

Mike went out of his way to make sure I felt welcome, picking up this country bumpkin right at the airport gate (back when that was still allowed). He spotted me as soon as I stepped off the plane and managed not to chuckle too loudly when I grabbed my luggage off of the baggage claim carousel, broken suit bag and all. When I asked Mike what he remembered about picking me up at the airport, he said, "That broken suit bag!" We'd never met before, but I knew it was him the moment I saw him: a bold alpha male ready to take me under his wing at the new station. He was only a few years older than me and soon became like a big brother. And, certainly, my biggest fan.

As the only soul I happened to know in this town, I moved into the same apartment complex as Mike. I was grateful to have him nearby both at work and at home. Of course, I'd moved around a lot in Seattle, changing neighborhoods, but this time there would be no mission president or companion in my little bachelor pad, just me, and for the first time in my life I had to figure things out without that built-in support network. At least if I lost my keys, I could knock on Mike's door!

The Dark Side

Part of doing radio in a bigger market like Orlando is being out there, among the listeners, doing promotional events and building your brand. Every Saturday night our station hosted a show at Sullivan's, a giant bar where five hundred to seven hundred country music fans heard live music, drank, and line danced. This fresh-faced Mormon boy wasn't used to the ruckus, but if I was to understand our listeners and this country music culture, I needed to dive in and be a part of it all. On one of those nights, I gave into temptation and had a beer, or three, or seven. I remember going to the restroom to pee, then feeling my first alcohol buzz.

Oh, so this is the feeling they're singing about in all those beer-drinking country music songs! I said to myself. I guess I needed to go over to the dark side to appreciate what the temptation was all about, and I can't say I hated it, not that it happened again for years. Luckily, Mike was around to make sure I got home okay.

Working at K-92 was the first time I experienced standing in front of an audience of thousands. We were hosting a George Strait concert at what was then known as the O-Rena (Orlando Arena), with a crowd of about eighteen thousand. Mike told me to go out onto the stage, welcome everyone, and introduce George. Backstage, my heart was in my throat. With thousands of people watching, I was terrified I might choke. My palms were sweaty, and my stomach was spasming as someone handed me the mic. But as soon as I walked out, the nerves disappeared. I felt completely at home. Bathed in the energy of thousands of country music fans, I said a few words to whip up their enthusiasm for the performance that was to come and got a taste of the euphoria artists must all feel as they stand in front of a live audience. It was like a drug, or maybe that recent beer buzz?

Working with Mike, I got to experience a lot of firsts. People started recognizing me around Orlando. Paul Williams, who was a marketing executive at the Universal Studios theme park, heard me one night and approached Mike about having me host a nationally syndicated weekend show. Also a radio industry veteran, Paul had an ear, and a clear idea of how his ideal country radio show should sound. Over the next few months, the three of us worked together on this passion project of ours and became the best of friends. When we weren't putting extra unpaid hours into brainstorming the show's potential, we were laughing at the crazy stories Mike and Paul shared about their lives in radio. I soaked up every word.

Also-Ran

About a year later, Dallas called. The general manager, Dan Halyburton at K-Plex, had heard me on a demo tape for the CMA Awards and decided I was the new blood they needed. On one level it was a no-brainer: triple the market, triple the salary. I wanted to prove myself, obviously, but I still took time to ponder the decision. I canvassed the opinions of a handful of people in the industry I'd met and respected.

"Why would you do that?" one of them asked me. "It's going to be a battle for a losing station that will never be anything but third place!"

My station in Orlando was number one. I could be a big fish and not take that risk.

Yeah, I thought to myself, *but maybe I can help win that battle.*

I wanted to be in a bigger market, even though I might fail. The hardest part was telling Mike, who was reluctant to let me go.

After a few chats and days to consider, he relented. "I'd love for you to stay but I realize this is something you need to do," said Mike, who's now a genius program director for Cumulus Media, which owns radio stations across the country.

Paul was also understanding, even though it meant I would no longer be able to launch his show at Universal.

"Cody, you've got to do this!" he told me. "Dallas is a great place and it's a hell of an opportunity."

The fact that I was more than tripling my salary, from $20,000 a year, which I somehow managed to live on in Orlando, to $70,000, an actual living wage, was another incentive, but not the primary one. What drove me most was the chance to prove myself as a fresh young voice in the industry.

Of course, that meant starting all over again in a new place, and it wasn't long before I started missing Mike's friendship and support. Thank God I had someone like him in my corner, who thought I was the shit. Just having someone nod at you and say, "You can do this," is incredibly powerful. If you listen carefully to that positive reinforcement, it can stay in your cells and power your growth. Mike and Paul's belief in me gave me the gumption, helping me to build just enough of a foundation of self-confidence to get through what lay ahead.

Mean Girls

The Dallas station was in a pickle. You could feel the dysfunction when you walked into the place. There was no sense of being a team, and the station itself didn't have any identifiable brand. After starting out with a middle-of-the-road format in the '70s, it switched to country in the '80s, with the slogan, "Flex Your Plex." This was followed by some success, then years of flailing, with no conviction about the music they were playing. Meanwhile, I thought the veteran radio guys hated me, constantly pointing out how green I was. One DJ, who'd been in the business for forty years, started picking on me like one of the mean girls in middle school.

I was just starting my shift and he was ending his when he came out of the booth and said, "What's that bird's nest on the back of your head?"

One of the things I liked least about myself was the fact that I was going bald. By my early twenties my hairline was already receding, and I was getting thin at the crown, with just enough tuft to cover the bare scalp if you didn't look too closely. As anyone going through hair loss knows, seeing all those dead follicles in your comb can be traumatic. Pointing out this "defect" was just the thing to say if anyone wanted to make me feel crummy, the perfect start to my day. I laughed it off because I don't like confrontation, and I always try to be respectful, but it was a nasty remark intended to hurt.

It was one of several attempts to embarrass me and make me feel less than. It wasn't long before I started hearing thirdhand that some of the old guard didn't like me. No one said it to my face, but there were rumblings that I didn't fit in at the station. I felt completely alone, with nothing but my four-hour shift from 3:00 to 7:00 p.m., prime-time driving, with millions of people listening.

Becoming Cody

Despite these early humiliations, it was at this point in my career that I was really beginning to find my voice. I was becoming Cody Alan, the on-air name I'd chosen for myself when I first moved to Dallas. Unfortunately, I was not born with a sexy name like Ryan Seacrest. Alan Chavis does not exactly trip off the tongue and besides, it's common for radio personalities to go by stage names. In Orlando, Mike Moore and I went through the phone book and came up with Cody McCoy. We sat in the conference room for a couple of hours, writing down my favorite first names and my favorite last names on a whiteboard, then cross paired. Cody sounded country, and it happened to be the name of a friend from childhood whose swagger I admired.

But I never loved McCoy. The combination of names made me feel like a cartoon character, or a guy from a spaghetti Western movie walking around with boot spurs and a ten-gallon hat. Besides, there happened to be another Cody McCoy on radio in the Dallas area, so the name had to change. I asked my new program director if I could change it to Cody Alan so that at least I'd still have some semblance of my real name. It felt right, and it stuck.

Meanwhile, I'd cultivated relationships with new mentors, like K-Plex program director Smokey Rivers, who took a risk when he hired me. Both he and GM Dan Halyburton had my back and taught me how to be a great on-air talent. They led by example, and I studied their approach, which would serve me later in my career when I had opportunities to do my own radio station programming. Finding these folks was just a matter of tuning out my detractors and hearing what mattered most.

Morning Zoo

Months after joining the K-Plex crew, I was paired with Stacey Brooks to do the morning show. In radio, morning and afternoon radio jocks tend to be two different beasts. The morning hosts create their own crazy universe, with plenty of fun on-air bits with banter and phone callers. The world rotates around them and everyone is in their orbit. They are characters, or caricatures of themselves, on the air to perform and be heard. They do crank calls to entertain the drivers stuck in traffic. Sometimes they are shock jocks and comedians, in the vein of Howard Stern, although he is in his own league. When they're good, they're brilliant, like Elvis Duran. It's pure entertainment.

At the time, I was much more of an afternoon drive guy. My sweet spot then was taking requests from listeners, making them feel like I'm communing with them one-on-one, overlaying our conversation with the music and a smile. I felt my approach was less about me sharing self-absorbed quips and more about the lives of the people listening. I wanted to create a sense of intimacy between the music, my listeners, and me. So the change in shift forced me to stretch and grow.

Of course, I wanted a shot at that prime-time morning spot. In radio, it's often the morning jocks who are the stars because they have that captive morning-drive audience. But aside from having to get up at 3:15 a.m., I had to learn how to carry on an hours-long conversation, bouncing off my cohost in a way that was witty, fun, and authentic. To our listeners, it had to sound easy, like two colleagues sharing effortless banter at the office over coffee and doughnuts.

But I was always on, wired and worried as I thought about the next topic, or how I was going to come up with the next spontaneous witticism. I wanted to prove I'd got this, but damn it was hard at only twenty-three! Stacey was generous, easing me into my talkative new role by lobbing softballs at me until it felt natural; doing all she could to make me look good. I was intimidated by what a pro she was at the morning radio banter and never quite felt her equal, but if Stacey ever felt I wasn't up to the task, she never showed it.

There were stumbles. When Ellen DeGeneres famously came out in April 1997 in *Time* magazine with the headline, "Yep, I'm Gay," the station management decided it would be a good idea for Stacey and me to have a debate on the air about the subject. Stacey would be pro Ellen coming out, and I would be against. We reflected the conversations a lot of our listeners were having across the nation, which was much more conservative and homophobic a quarter century ago. Deep in the closet as I was, I assumed the fake role of homophobe and duly criticized the woman who was to become one of my all-time greatest heroes. It felt icky, and now I can't look back on the incident without cringing. Just because I was playing the game, pretending to play a character with an opinion, didn't make it right.

Mistakes are inevitable. Few people can look back on the sweep of their careers without moments of regret. But I was lucky, because it happened in the days before Twitter and social media could amplify every misstep. A bad choice or an off moment didn't have to ruin you back then. Folks in the public eye weren't subjected to the level of scrutiny we're seeing today. We're all human; we all have off days. Even Ellen, one of the kindest people on television, took heat when it was leaked that things behind the scenes didn't meet the stringent standards she'd set for herself. Although my profile is nowhere near as high as Ellen's, I know what that pressure to be constantly "on" feels like. That's why I make it a point not to listen when others in the spotlight face an avalanche of disapproval. There but for the grace of God go I.

Little did I know then that, twenty years later in my life, I would meet Ellen. It was in Santa Barbara, California, at a fundraiser for wildfire victims she was hosting, along with Brad Paisley. Over a couple of Modelo beers, I took the opportunity to tell her how much I appreciated her coming out, and how it had helped me and countless others. I'm sure she hears it all the time, but I didn't care. I wanted her to know how I felt. After my gushing gratitude, I said to her, "I'm gay!" And she enthusiastically said, "Me too!" with a big smile.

Turnaround Ace

Back to Texas in 1998—rumors were swirling that we were all about to lose our jobs, due to the station's low ratings. Susquehanna Radio, the company that owned K-Plex, wanted a complete makeover of the station. They were hoping to make it to the number two spot in Dallas, which would finally bring the kind of listening audience and ad sales necessary to survive. So, in the summer of 1998, they brought in their star program director from Atlanta, Brian Philips, a guy known for aggressively turning around music stations.

Brian's previous stations played Top 40 pop and rock, so the scuttlebutt was that he planned to change our format, which probably meant getting rid of all us country DJs. With the real possibility of being kicked to the curb, I'd already been casting around for a new gig and was offered a spot at a leading country music station in Nashville, WSIX. They even flew me to meet with everyone. I was dazzled by the place. They showed me around town and pointed to the houses where my music heroes lived. I spent time with the head of the new show and met my potential cohost, a very cool woman who was already a Nashville insider. We went to a local bar and played pool together. It was my first time playing and I felt so uncoordinated. Although I was flattered by their attention, they thought it was pretty much a done deal by the time they dropped me off at the airport. But to me, something about the whole experience felt forced.

Was this really the right decision? I wondered. I loved the life I'd built in Dallas and was reluctant to leave, but I wasn't so sure I had a choice. For someone whose two greatest loves were country and radio, getting a show curating country music in the industry's mecca, just three years into my radio career, was a dream come true. Plus, they would double my salary again! I should have been overjoyed.

I hardly knew Brian, who'd only been at his desk for a couple of weeks before I walked into his office to tell him my news.

"Hey, Brian, I have this contract sitting on my kitchen table, waiting to be signed. But I love Texas. What should I do?"

"You should stay," he told me.

Brian planned to fire almost all the on-air talent. That's how he approached the turnaround. It would mean letting go of some good people, but they weren't projecting the kind of energy and excitement he was looking for. Some were too identified with the previous version of the station, while others weren't open to change. But there was something about me he liked and felt would be a fit for the revamped programming. He wasn't necessarily impressed with the job I was doing in my morning slot, but he instinctively understood that it wasn't my best fit and liked the fact that I was young and energetic. He'd also spoken with Paul Williams, an old friend of his from back when Paul worked in radio, and my old friend from Universal Studios in Orlando.

"Cody's a good kid, you're gonna love him," he assured Brian.

Brian took the time to explain his vision for the station's re-launch. It would stay country. Instead of relying on heavy rotation of the same country songs that were being played over the previous decade, he wanted to bring some edge, taking a risk on new artists, especially those red dirt Texas artists that local listeners loved but weren't being taken as seriously by the country music gods in Nashville. I'd be encouraged to curate the music I believed in, from any era, and discover the new, with an emphasis on raucous guitar-heavy songs that would appeal to younger, mostly male listeners like me. The hope was that we could recapture the eighteen- to thirty-four-year-olds who'd drifted over to Top 40. Brian told me he wasn't content with just being the number two station. He wanted to be number one. He was planning to launch an all-out attack to dominate the market and change Dallas–Fort Worth radio as we knew it. He told me how they were going to spend big money on billboards and TV ads, and how he wanted me to be a part of something that was going to be bigger and better.

"Cody, there is something about you that defines what this new station is going to be about. I love your ear, the way you talk to listeners, and your offbeat comedic timing. You have that feel for Texas Country we need. If you're willing to go back to the afternoon time slot, I will take care of you."

Brian was full of charisma and conviction. Before the conversation was over, he made me a believer and, when I got home that night, I tore up the Nashville contract. Moving to Nashville would have been the logical move. They made it clear how much they wanted me and were even willing to pay my expenses for the move. There were no guarantees that what Brian had in mind would work, and he was even asking me to accept a demotion of sorts by moving out of the morning drive show, where I was head of my own small ensemble cast, including the best news reporter in radio, Chris Sommer, and the *mucho* talented Stacey. But Brian could have told me to run into a burning house and I'd have done it. I could sense his decency and dedication. And I believed him, even accepting much less pay than Nashville was offering me. Six figures less! But money wasn't my goal (ever). I've always been more prone to following my heart instead of my head and made that leap into the unknown with him.

Texas Country

The transition from K-Plex to "The Wolf" was one heck of an undertaking. A lot of thought went into our rebranding. For weeks, we researched Texas country music, from the biggest stars like George Strait to the more outside-the-lines artists like Robert Earl Keen. Brian ordered Paul Koffy, a newly hired jock who couldn't go on air until the relaunch, to gather up all the biographical information he could on the artists we would be playing. He wanted us all to know their stories backward and forward. Of course, this was before Google, so Paul went to the local library to look up articles and compile information on every Texas musician he could find. He made hard copies of everything he dug up, stapled each bio together, and created a Trapper Keeper–like file folder for each of us. I am not sure if he intended it to be a joke, but each pink pastel folder was decorated with kittens, like something a little girl would have on her first day of class in grade school. Paul, who became a great friend and now does a nationally syndicated radio show out of Nashville, has been "Kitten Boy" to me ever since.

Brian kept most of the planning under wraps. We didn't even know what the new station would be called because he didn't want to risk the information coming out until the day of the launch, to deprive the other stations in town the opportunity to make fun of us. Shortly before the big day, there was a dinner with Dan and Brian. Dan took out a napkin and drew what looked like a paw. "The Mark of the Paw" would become our most recognizable piece of branding. It was there every time we had an event. When people saw that paw print, they knew they'd be in for a great time with The Wolf, with awesome prizes and great music.

On launch day, on a Friday afternoon about an hour before the first show came on air, Brian decided to play the instrumental theme from the movie soundtrack of *Dances with Wolves*. He wanted to create a sense of mystery and build up suspense, but for some longtime listeners, it had the opposite effect. Back then, we had these clunky old beige push-button phones in the producer's room, with four lights to indicate when someone was on the line. The entire time we were playing that music, all the phones were lit up as people called in to complain.

"Have y'all switched formats?" one of them asked.

"Are you an easy listenin' station now?" said another.

Uh-oh, I thought. But I felt strongly that what was to come would be the most exciting relaunch of a station in radio history.

Then, finally, we went live, launching "The All New 99.5, The Wolf." Often when a new station launches or relaunches, the first song played is a theme song that evokes the new approach. Such was the case with The Wolf, as our first song became our new anthem. It was Robert Earl Keen's "The Road Goes On Forever."

Once we officially launched, the DJs each had forty-five minutes to introduce themselves on air between songs. I went on at around 6:20 p.m., after The Wolf had been live for an hour or so. It was a moment I felt I'd been practicing for my whole life, from the time I played with Mr. Microphone in my room. Like an Olympic swimmer about to jump off the high diving board, I was exposed in nothing but a metaphorical banana hammock. I had nothing more than a fifteen-second song intro to prove myself. I felt like it was my chance to jump off the high dive and do some twirls.

"This is The Wolf, Texas Country," I said on my first live break, before introducing a Dixie Chicks song and enthusiastically welcoming listeners to our newfound sound as Cody Alan, a guy I hoped they knew and liked. I felt good about my delivery, which was crisp and fresh. I was showing off my chops as best I could, excitedly accepting the new phraseology of the station, and what would become a long and awesome new phase in my life. While the song was playing, Brian came running down the hallway and barged into the studio.

"Who did that last break?" Brian asked to the crowd of staff amassed in the studio.

Oh shit, I messed up, I thought to myself. *Couldn't he tell it was me?*

I raised my hand and confessed, "It was me."

"That!" he said, pointing at me. "That is exactly what I want!"

We spent the rest of that night spinning records that hadn't been heard on the radio ever before, mixed with classics from familiar favorites like Willie Nelson and Waylon Jennings. In time, we discovered and exposed listeners to artists like Pat Green, Cross Canadian Ragweed, Randy Rogers Band, and Jack Ingram. Our clever music brand was to blend the best of Texas Country and Nashville's mainstream hits from Tim McGraw, Kenny Chesney, and even Shania Twain.

At first, not everyone was as enthused about what we were presenting to our listeners. The *Dallas Morning News* wrote a scathing review of the relaunch, calling it a terrible mistake. Poor Brian was distraught. There are those who have a tough time embracing change, even when the status quo sucks. But soon people started to get it. The whole experience reminds me of the quote from Elon Musk, "Good ideas are always crazy until they're not." People don't always know what they want until you show them what they need.

Brian hired Paul Williams, again our mutual friend from Orlando, to help with the marketing. In another stroke of pure genius, Brian hired the Emmy Award–winning actor Barry Corbin as our station's voice. Barry was a true Texan who lived on a working ranch just outside of Dallas. Best known for his roles in the miniseries *Lonesome Dove* and the television show *Northern Exposure*, Barry had a deep, rich voice and a Texan drawl that put you in a place. When he said something, you believed it. We gave him these one-liners in between songs like, "I'd rather be a fence post in Texas than the king of Tennessee," and "This. Is. Texas Country!"

In one of our promos. he read "The Creedo of The Wolf" to a background of haunting music and howling wolves with dramatic flair:

Respect the elders
Teach the young
Cooperate with the pack
Play when you can
Hunt when you must
Rest in between
Share your affections
Voice your feelings
Leave your mark
The new 99.5 . . . The Wolf.

Barry was describing the way a happy wolf pack functions, and that's exactly what we were. While Brian had kept me, Smokey Rivers, and Chris Sommer from the old guard, he'd assembled a mostly brand-new team of the best radio people from across the country: Top 40 veteran Bobby Mitchell, Texas spitfire talent Tara and Jon "Mr. Leonard" Rio on our morning show, "Kitten Boy" Paul Koffey, and, finally, Amy B., one of the most entertaining phone jocks ever on the radio. Of course, there was the occasional mild sibling rivalry, but The Wolf was first and foremost a family.

Barry also did riffs for every on-air event, "Howl-a'ween" specials, "Wolfathon" twelve-in-a-row music blocks, and our annual St. Jude Children's Hospital "Hunt for a Cure" for which we raised more than one million dollars in two days, every year. We were no longer just musical wallpaper to our Dallas listeners, something that just played in the background for office workers. The Wolf imagery, along with Barry's voice, was catching. Our listeners could visualize what we were all about: that proud Texan vibe. We ruffled some feathers, bashing the Nashville sound to get some attention, even though we of course played many Nashville songs. But we were all about that rebellious Texas spirit.

Another new Wolf hire was Brett "Dingo" O'Brien, a twenty-year-old radio nerd with a wicked smart marketing mind, who'd moved to Texas from Australia when he was fifteen; hence the nickname. Dingo was originally hired to help produce the morning show and he fit into The Wolf culture right away. For his twenty-first birthday, someone ran down to the nearest gas station to buy him his first six-pack of beer, which the morning crew made him drink on the air.

Dingo and I quickly discovered we were kindred spirits. We liked the same music, shared a similar sense of humor, and had the same marketing and branding background, so we knew how to package and sell what we loved. On the side, we produced a show I created, "The Country Now Countdown," an independent syndicated program. Once a week Dingo would come in and help me record the show. I'd order dinner, and we'd edit the show and burn it on CDs that we'd send out to various stations. It never made much money, so I paid Dingo what I could with a personal check. The real reward was hanging out together and building a lifelong friendship.

Blake Shelton remembers our countdown attempt. His song "Austin" once hit its top spot. To this day, whenever we chat, Blake brings up his gratitude for that first number one in Texas, and how our fledgling show gave his music credibility before the Nashville charts ever did.

Dingo was also a second pair of ears at The Wolf as I discovered new music, one of my greatest joys. We were one of the few remaining radio stations that were permitted to find and make our own hits. Each week, the record labels would send us a pile of CDs. But I didn't want some label's A&R guy curating records for me. These companies had their own agendas and weren't necessarily putting listeners first. They made calculations about what was commercial in the past, which often left no room for what was new, fresh, edgy, or worthy of The Wolf's high standards, which I termed "Wolf-a-licious."

Ear Candy

A great Wolf song was generally a rollicking, guitar-heavy Texas sound, loud and proud and fun. We took risks on songs that were completely overlooked by the other stations, like "Horse to Mexico" by Trini Triggs and "Barlight" by Charlie Robison. We played songs by young artists who were often completely disdained by other purveyors of country music, like "I'm Diggin' It" by Alecia Elliott, who was just seventeen in 2000, the year we put it into rotation. We also made hits happen nationally for other non-Texans, like Mark McGuinn's ear candy song "Mrs. Steven Rudy." Texan artists were often at the front of the line, but not always.

One day I dug a CD out of the pile. It was by a band called The Ranch, and it was as Wolf-a-licious as anything I'd ever heard. I played it for Brian.

"I don't know, Cody," Brian said. "It rocks like Texas, and the guitar sound is intriguing, but it's kinda out of left field."

"I think they're going to be huge," I told him. "Let's play it!"

The Ranch was Keith Urban's band, long before anyone had heard of Keith Urban, and certainly not the Keith Urban now married to Nicole Kidman. But we put one of The Ranch's songs on, called "Walkin' the Country," and once again it was on-air magic.

Another radio rule we broke was not limiting ourselves to light rotations if we liked something. We played the bejesus out of our favorites: every hour and a half until they caught on. They were the songs that we could not get enough of, and they ultimately defined us. It also happened to be what our Texas listeners were hungry for at that moment.

Of course, not all the records I picked were loud bar songs for cowboys to stomp to. Again, I sifted through another record label batch and found this sweet ballad. It was about a mother's wish for her daughter to live her life to the fullest, by an artist who was critically acclaimed but still lacked that breakthrough song. Again, I played it for Brian, who cocked his head in confusion.

"Yeah, Cody, the melody is beautiful, I love her voice, and the artist is from Texas, but it sounds like a wedding song. Is this us? Is it Wolf-a-licious?"

"Brian, it's going to be song of the year," I told him. One of the things that I think Brian liked about me is I always told him how I felt, even if he disagreed. Luckily, if I feel strongly enough that I'm right, I feel confident speaking up, even if it means putting my neck on the line.

Of course, the song was Lee Ann Womack's "I Hope You Dance." The chorus just soared, and the lyrics pierced the heart. It resonated with me, especially as a new Girl Dad. I could imagine a time when I would have that same conversation with my own daughter, only Lee Ann said it better than I ever could. That's why I wasn't surprised that, a year later, Lee Ann Womack went on to win 2001 Song of the Year at the CMAs, ACMs, and more.

I spent a decade at The Wolf, which is a long time in radio years, much like dog years, I think. What kept me there for so long, besides my love for Texas and the roots I put down in Dallas, was the fact that I was able to take on multiple roles. In addition to being an afternoon jock, Brian asked me to be a music director and programmer. I'll never forget the conversation about taking The Wolf's musical reins, since it was my birthday, November 13. He had no idea of the serendipity of that moment. (The same birthday coincidence would happen years later at CMT on another November 13, when Brian asked me if I would host the soon-to-be-rebranded Top 20 video countdown show.)

There were so many memorable career milestones, including the first time I felt like a celebrity. I'd always been the guy who, before I met my wife, did my show, put it in a box on the shelf, then went home to a dinky apartment. But all of a sudden, at the Smirnoff Music Center during one of our Amphitheater concerts, I couldn't even walk through the crowd. I was constantly being stopped by people asking for my autograph or to pose for pictures with me or meet the rest of their family. One or two people would spot me, and soon there'd be a line of people. The closest I had come to that level of attention was representing a station at some sort of auto dealership prize wheel spin. All of the on-air personalities at The Wolf were getting recognized; we were that successful in the Dallas–Fort Worth market. It was fun and flattering, although the rush of people at our events could be a little daunting at times.

In 2005, I even got to do mornings again, which turned out much better because by then I had improved on-air reflexes from my years at The Wolf. Professionally, the experience taught me that when you have the courage not to play anyone else's game but your own, you will excel. Again, it was the road less traveled. A few people got upset with the station, and me, because we didn't play by the rules. But they also admired us. We weren't trying to be different for its own sake. We just wanted to be authentic, so we took calculated risks and followed our gut. We were total mavericks, and that put us on a winning streak.

In 2007, I left on a high note. I was growing restless and decided it was time for a new challenge, running my own station as a program director in Salt Lake City, Utah. The payoffs from listening to my inner voice and taking a chance had built up my confidence to the point where I was ready to take that next huge leap.

• THE STANDARD BEARER •

by Brian Philips

WHEN I FIRST ARRIVED IN Dallas, my initial reaction was to just get rid of everybody and start over. When you're coming in from the outside to turn around a radio station, it's just easier that way. The old staff are gone before you walk in the door so that you don't form attachments. It enables you to do what's got to be done without feeling rotten about it and risking the makeover. In a mercenary way I was hungry for fast change and growth. But after spending some time in the building, I was glad we were doing it the hard way, because it gave me a chance to listen to Cody.

He was a natural talent. Our goal was to build a more vibrant and youthful product, and Cody fit that bill. Beyond that, I loved the way he talked to listeners on the phone, which is a rare and prized radio skill. He was also a master of offbeat, comedic timing. He displayed a humility, humor, and curiosity about others that made his callers the stars. We had a red phone hotline inside the studio so that, as program director, I could call in even while Cody was on air. I kept calling in to say, "Do more of that!" Cody understood the country music audience at an intuitive level, and still does. Between his repartee with listeners, his gregarious personality, and his innate understanding of the spirit of Texas Country, he defined what I was trying to do at The Wolf. He became the standard bearer.

I knew he could re-create the same level of magic when I hired him at CMT years later. Although I admit, I had no idea he would end up being a great TV host too! But Cody is and has always been a conscientious and hard worker, a consummate showman, and a gifted broadcaster who understands the many aspects of the business.

TEXAS BOMBSHELL

And I turn into the guy with the girl everybody wants to know.
—BLAKE SHELTON, "A Guy with a Girl"

She was a little tipsy, and I was a lot late.

My first date with Terresa almost didn't happen. I got lost on the way to Joe's Crab Shack, and it was a while before I realized I had been driving in the opposite direction on 635. We decided to meet at Joe's, a cheesy family-style seafood chain, because it was halfway between Dallas, where I lived, and Fort Worth, near where she lived with her parents. I was horrified that the poor girl might think she was being stood up—that's not how I was raised—so I pulled over to a pay phone to call the restaurant and beg whoever picked up the phone at the bar to let her know. By then Terresa had already been sitting at the table for almost an hour. The waiter took pity on her and kept sending over drinks compliments of the house. I guess it took the sting out of the humiliation because, by the time I finally arrived full of apologies, she greeted me with a dazzling smile.

It was a blind date arranged by a mutual friend. Well, blind in a one-sided sort of way. It was 1997 and I'd already been working at K-Plex Radio, The Wolf's precursor, for several months, so I was already a familiar name and voice on the Dallas–Fort Worth scene. Terresa already knew about me because I used to talk about my life on the radio. We had met a couple of times before in passing, but my memory of those encounters is hazy. I was working a live concert event in the parking lot of a local Walmart attended by Terresa and her four-year-old daughter, Lauren, and we exchanged brief hellos, or so she reminded me. A few of the DJs were there to meet and greet fans and listeners. Another time, Terresa was among a handful of people who'd won a birthday lunch with listeners, but we sat on opposite ends of the table. Again, she had to remind me of that fact.

Terresa was a huge country music fan and an avid listener of the local country radio stations, especially mine. She was always calling in to win prizes for the various contests we had, attending events on concerts we hosted whenever she could. The girl also had hustle. She was doing some work for the Fort Worth Fire hockey team and approached Chris Sommer, our morning news guy, to see if we could do ticket giveaways to the games. The two bantered back and forth, starting up a friendly little email correspondence.

"That Cody is such a cutie," she told him.

"Well, he's single," Chris wrote back, then decided to play Cupid by telling me about my admirer.

Early the following Saturday morning, Terresa was taking a computer class and I happened to be on the radio. She called in to make a song request, we got to chatting off air, and I finally made the connection.

"Is this the Terresa I saw the other night with the little girl?" I asked her.

"Yes, that's me! Well, you don't know me yet, but I sure do remember you!" she said.

I got up the nerve to ask her for her number. Because she was living at her family home, she didn't want to give it to me in case one of her protective parents answered the phone, so, in the days before cell phones were commonplace, she gave me her pager number. Yes, her pager! Google it—it was quite a device. We had a few more phone conversations before I finally got up the nerve to ask her on a date. I knew nothing about her, other than that she was a sweet, wholesome, age-appropriate girl who happened to be a single mom to a little girl. But here's what I learned about her by the time we closed down the crab shack:

Terresa is petite. At just 5'2" she's the perfect Texan doll in her jeans and cowboy boots. In fact, she was the kind of girl all the boys in high school would have fallen for, but who I'd never have imagined would look at me twice. And yet here she was, laser focused on yours truly with those high-beamed blue eyes of hers. I was beyond flattered, and I must admit that I was already beginning to fall in love with how we looked together as a couple. In high school I was no jock, nor did I have the height and sculpted body of the football-playing types all the girls went for. But Terresa's femininity made me feel like a manly man.

Seductive Listener

She was also bubbly, fearless, and fun to be around. Even though the thought of sexual attention from anyone, male or female, terrified me, something about this small-town country girl's sense of humor and flirtatiousness put me right at ease. She also seemed genuinely interested in what I had to say. Her undivided attention made me feel like that guy in the beer ad, "the most interesting man in the world." You can tell a lot about someone's potential compatibility in a relationship by how intently they listen.

A down-home Texas girl who came from an old ranching family in San Angelo, Texas, Terresa had a sense of adventure. She could ride horses, shoot a gun, drive a tractor, and hold her own on a mechanical bull. She was not afraid to get her hands dirty, and she was most comfortable in scuffed-up boots and faded jeans. But she could also dance, do up her hair and makeup like a beauty queen, and turn heads. Terresa had married her college sweetheart, Lauren's father, and moved to Houston, but when the relationship fell apart, she returned home, taking jobs from waitressing to admin to support herself and her child because, "I've been working since I was fourteen years old and I want to get back on my own two feet."

Aside from her first husband, Terresa had never dated. At twenty-four, less than a year older than I was, she obviously had some sexual experience whereas I, of course, had none, zero, zilch. She also came from a religious family, Southern Baptists like mine, but even bigger churchgoers than my mom, because they attended services on most weeknights. Her parents were salt-of-the-earth types who rode horses to school when they were kids. They met in the fifth grade and have been together ever since. They doted on Terresa and accepted anyone who Terresa loved as one of their own, as long she was happy.

It was immediately obvious to me that Terresa had a nurturing soul. She knew how to listen with her whole being. Until then, I'd always felt like I was the listener, the person in the room who could draw someone out of their shell with my charm. But Terresa got me to share things about myself I'd never told anyone else—everything except that I liked men, which I wasn't even telling myself at this point. With her, I became the talker. And it stemmed from the fact that I knew she genuinely wanted to know every detail she could about me. For the first time, as I stood on the other side of the conversation, I understood viscerally the power that a great listener has to seduce!

That night at Joe's we talked nonstop for a good four hours, delving into our stories and what made us tick until they had to throw us out of there. I ordered a Blue Moon beer and pretended to nurse it because, although I was a Mormon and didn't drink, I wanted Terresa to feel comfortable enough to sip another margarita and keep the conversation going. The connection felt so natural and comfortable, it was almost as if we were old friends from a past life, and I didn't want the evening to end. The restaurant was one of those places where you could write on the table. They even provided you with a marker. That night we wrote our names down among all the other couples' names and love hearts, and as far as I know they are still there. Even then I kinda knew I'd met my future wife.

We were more or less inseparable from that moment on. I took Terresa to concerts and work parties all over the metroplex, and it was as much fun driving down the highway in my two-door Ford Explorer, laughing, talking, and making plans for our future as it was hanging out with the country stars and fans once we got to our destination. On weekends and evenings, I would hang out with her at the family homestead where Terresa, her folks, and I drank beers to wash down some Tex-Mex, while neighbors, cousins, uncles, and aunts stopped by to tell jokes and gossip. I loved that warm hug of acceptance.

But at one point I started to feel overwhelmed. It was all happening so fast. I was falling hard not just for Terresa, but Lauren, and before I thought I was ready to wrap my head around it, I was already taking on a fatherly role to a little girl who'd only been in my life for a short time. It was almost frightening how protective I felt for her, but was I even qualified? I'd only recently lost my virginity to Terresa and now this. *Whoa!* I thought. *What am I getting myself into?*

If I was going to be a stepdad and have an instant family, I wanted to be sure I was all in. I pumped the breaks and told Terresa I needed a monthlong pause before taking the relationship any further. Retreating into my own space is something I've always done when I felt some kind of turmoil. I need to be still and turn inward to hear my own voice. Of course, Terresa was sweet and understanding about it, as she always was. She appreciated the fact that I didn't want to have any doubts about our future together and risk breaking two hearts. Or three, if I count my own.

Country Star Competition

A week or so before our "time-out," we attended a Gary Allan concert together. We were both huge fans, and Terresa was starstruck when we went backstage. I didn't think much of it at the time, but I noticed Gary was being especially attentive to Terresa.

Fresh off his debut gold album, *Used Heart for Sale*, as well as his first marriage, Gary was doing multiple performances in the Dallas–Fort Worth area. So, when the opportunity came up two weeks later to attend another concert at Billy Bob's, the world's largest honky-tonk, Terresa decided to take advantage of her temporary single status to go out and have herself some fun with one of her girlfriends. She found herself sitting in the front row, where Gary recognized her, grabbed her camera, and took a pre-selfie selfie. He flirted with her through the rest of the performance. As Terresa was leaving, one of Gary's managers pulled her aside.

"Gary wants to meet you," he told her.

"But I already met him," she said.

"He wants you to stay."

"Sorry, I've got to get home to my daughter."

"Can he at least have your number?"

"Sorry, I don't give out my number."

A few days later, as Terresa was pulling up the driveway of her parents' home after work, her mom came running out to the car.

"Gary Allan's on the phone for you!"

Terresa was rushing to get her daughter, Lauren, ready for cheerleading practice, so she was slightly annoyed as she picked up the phone, wondering which of her friends was pulling a prank. But it really was Gary, calling from Salt Lake City where his ex-wife lived, visiting his kids.

"How in the world did you get my number?" she asked him.

"Your friend gave it to me," he told her, declining to specify which friend.

Gary invited her to another concert, this time in Killeen, Texas, more than a two-hour drive south. Terresa drove there with another girlfriend and, when they arrived, they got the VIP treatment, hanging out on the bus and drinking beers with the bandmates. Gary, who is a good-looking California dude with the swagger of a rock star, did his best to impress. Luckily for me, Terresa was oblivious.

"He must have thought I was such a music dork," Terresa told me later, convinced that, to him, she was nothing more than a fan.

Although we were on a break, we were still communicating. She called to ask me if I was the one who gave him her number. As if! Suddenly I felt competitive, and the four-week break was cut short at two weeks. I was always serious about Terresa, but now I knew I had to up my game before she was stolen from me. I must have interviewed him more than a hundred times since, but I never mentioned the fact that he tried courting my girl! No one knew, until now.

Instant Family

Soon after Terresa and I got back together, I decided it was time for us to take it to the next level. I found an apartment big enough for the three of us in Irving, less than a twenty-minute commute from work.

"I have a surprise for you," I told her on the way there, dropping silly hints about what that might be. "It has cows."

"Are we going to the stock show?" she asked, showing her "Texas" as she genuinely thought this was a possibility.

When we arrived at the condos, Terresa squealed. Not only was she thrilled to be getting out from under the watchful eyes of her parents, but our new home happened to be across the street from where her beloved Dallas Cowboys practiced.

Terresa got pregnant soon after we moved in together. We had a shotgun wedding in front of a justice of the peace. She didn't care about a big wedding because she'd already had one the first time around, but she was worried I'd feel like I was missing out. As far as I was concerned, I'd already won the prize: an adorable little family that could grace the filler photos they use to sell picture frames.

Terresa also graced me with a willingness to embrace the Mormon faith. Having been raised in a religious family, similar to me, it wasn't such a huge leap for Terresa to accept a different set of miracles. She did her own research and made her own decisions about what she believed. She approached the whole conversion process with humility and an open mind, telling herself, *My way is not always the right way, so let's see.*

Her parents, like mine, had concerns, but, as she put it, "They know I am a grown-ass woman and if I felt it was not right, I would not do it."

As much as she embraced my faith and supported my career with her whole being, Terresa was always her own woman. She didn't need to, but she insisted on working. We had only one car, which I needed to drive to the station, so she found a job at a Mexican restaurant in a strip mall down the road that was a walkable distance and worked there before and after our daughter Makayla was born, working the lunch shift while a neighbor watched the baby. Not long after giving birth, she also got it into her head to try out for the Dallas Cowboy cheerleaders, which had long been a dream of hers. She almost made the team.

A few years later, we built our own dream home in the suburbs. By then Terresa was pregnant with our second child, Landon, and motherhood became her full-time occupation, taking the kids to and from school, dance practice, and little league games. My career at The Wolf was taking off, our family was growing, and our life had settled into a satisfying rhythm of love, faith, and work.

Being a parent became my greatest joy. Landon was my Mini-Me who shared my passions, from his near-obsessive collection of Matchbox cars as a little boy, to his ear for music. But I was in awe of Makayla's dainty girlishness. Terresa always made sure the girls were dressed in the cutest outfits. Everything about Makayla was immaculate, from her brunette hair to her pretty pink fingernails. She was *my* little ball of sunshine. All three of our kids were the gifts Terresa gave me.

On the radio, everyone knew me as that family guy. I was always talking about my kids. I shared how Makayla was filled with energy, always giggling. She brought the electricity to our family from the first time she opened her eyes. One of my most famous "bits" that we incorporated into our radio format was a phone-in contest called "What's Landon Saying?," based on recordings of my two-year-old son's incomprehensible streams of toddler-ese. Again, with the dad-joke humor!

People often ask me how, as a gay man, I could possibly have been happy in a straight marriage. There is only one answer to that question: Terresa. This beer-drinking, horse-riding, country-music-loving Texas blonde bombshell was the only woman I could ever imagine building a life with. Of course, I was fresh off my Mormon mission, so I had marriage on the brain. The Mormons believe that being married brings you closer to God, and I had hoped it would change me and make me 100 percent right in God's eyes. But I couldn't have made it work with just anyone. Terresa was perfect for me in every way because we shared the same values. She had a generosity of spirit that put others first, me especially. If only everyone could experience having a person in their lives who is all the above.

Don't get me wrong, we also had real chemistry. It wasn't exactly the kind where you lock eyes with someone across the room and are overcome with desire, at least not for me. I've only ever experienced that kind of passion with a man. But human sexuality is fluid and complicated. We don't all fit in a specific box. Having someone be that attracted to you can be a turn-on in its own way. Terresa always made me feel safe and unconditionally loved. Despite my lack of experience, doubts, and fears, I couldn't resist her charms.

Against the odds, I'd created a life with a loving, accepting, and supportive partner who built up my confidence with a devotion I never imagined possible. Anyone who meets Terresa immediately understands why it took me so long to leave her, even though I knew I was gay. She is that special, and I have thanked God every day for bringing her into my life. The kid in high school who never thought he could get or deserve a loving woman, much less a beauty with a heart bigger than Texas, kept playing the movie in his head, and it was as close to perfect as it could be.

• A DOTING DAD, PART I •

by Makayla, Cody's daughter

FIRST OFF, I HAVE THE coolest dad in the world. From my earliest childhood in Texas to church life in Salt Lake, to my young adult life in Nashville, I have nothing but happy memories.

He is so caring. He'd drop anything to do anything for anyone. Growing up Mormon meant there were rules, of course, and my father always made sure we understood the importance of working hard for what you want. But he always managed to teach us lessons in that "fun dad" way of his.

When I turned sixteen, he surprised me with the keys to his old Lexus. Dad loved that car, which he'd owned for ten years. He knew I'd always dreamed of driving it, but it wasn't long before I totaled it. I was driving home from dance class in the pouring rain, going fifteen miles per hour, when someone slammed the brakes in front of me, and I rear-ended them. I was sobbing, and I thought, *Dad is going to kill me!* But when he came to pick me up, he didn't even look at his car. All that mattered to him was that I was okay.

Soon after, Dad decided to buy me another car. I told him I would drive anything, but said, "Please don't make me drive a Corolla." Sure enough, it was a Corolla. When we pulled up to the bank parking lot, where my father picked up the money order to pay for the car, I screamed, "Noooooooo, Dad, noooooo!"

As I continued to whine, Dad chuckled, handed over the payment to the previous owner, then gave me the keys. Poor Landon had to drive that thing a few years later, after I finally got a new car. My father had a special fondness for this model. He's always been a big believer in their safety and reliability, ever since he had to drive an old rust-bucket Corolla when he was a teenager. But the message for me was clear: if I wanted something better, I'd have to earn it.

Over time, I actually grew to love that car. We still have it. We keep it in the driveway in case any of the family's other vehicles need servicing. We call her Carol. Carol the Corolla.

A legend.

((6))

CHURCH CLOTHES

But we smile and we give it our Sunday best
If we're lost couldn't tell by the way we dressed.
—KELLEIGH BANNEN, "Church Clothes"

Deep in the heart of Texas, I had everything a man could ask for in life: a great career full of professional accolades, two gorgeous children of my own, an incredible stepdaughter, and a beautiful Texas bride. The birth of Makayla, my pretty little angel, and soon after, Landon, the Mini-Me I'd dreamed of, tied everything up into a perfect bow. I loved my job at The Wolf. It didn't even feel like a job, because I got to wake up every day and walk into a place where I was surrounded by dear friends who shared my passion and loved radio as much as I did. And Terresa's family, salt-of-the-earth oil-catters and ranchers, embraced me as one of their own. I'd put down solid Texas roots, to the point where my Wolf teammates would tease me that I was more Texan than most Texans in my boots and cowboy hat (any chance I could get to cover up my balding head). I felt like the Lone Star State's beloved adopted son.

But something was always missing. The comfort of my situation almost grated on me. I was never completely happy and felt guilty for it. How dare I reject these gifts. How could I not be content with all the blessings I had? Of course, I was faithful to my wife, provided for my family, did everything a good man is supposed to do, but I was filled with self-loathing because I knew that, deep down, I was faking it. It felt like slow suffocation. That attraction to men just wouldn't go away, no matter how hard I tried to stamp it down.

It all stemmed from the fact that I wasn't listening to myself. I'd spent a lifetime tuning out the voice within. Actually, it was worse than that. I didn't want to hear a peep, so I cut it off with external concerns like my career, fear for my reputation, and the desire to create a picture-perfect family life. After living this way for a while, you become resentful and angry, but you're never quite sure why. The simple joys don't exist for you because you are never really in the moment, and everything starts to feel like an obligation or a burden.

As a result, I was never fully present for the people I loved, using work as my escape route as I focused on one goal, and the next, until I'd finally hit a ceiling at The Wolf and all the goal posts were behind me. Some people are okay with staying in a groove, especially when they can enjoy all of life's other riches. Not me. I could never be at peace with myself, not just because the disconnect I felt between who I was and the life I was living, but because I was constantly dreaming up the next big thing. I was wired to seek out a challenge. There was nothing worse for me than sitting still. It put me into a panic. What next?

Yank my family away from the people and places they knew and loved and move to Salt Lake City, Utah, that's what.

Fairy Godfather

Not that seeking that distraction over the next horizon was my only motivation for leaving behind the life we'd built in Dallas. I'd always wanted to run my own station. I could see myself moving into the executive corner office. By the end of a decade at The Wolf, I'd tried out just about every position, giving me a good thirty-thousand-foot view of how all the pieces fit together. Just like when I was a kid, I played that movie in my head of how I would run a station and coach a morning show. So, when I heard that Simmons Media, a privately owned radio group based in Salt Lake City, Utah, had an opening at their station, The Eagle, I was determined to make it mine. At first, the guy who ran the operation told me I was overqualified for the job.

"Cody, why would you want to come to a smaller market like ours?"

I told him where my ambitions lay, and he could hear me brimming with confidence about all the things I believed I could do to kick some life into his station. I also explained I was a Mormon. I knew their audience because I was one of them. I was uniquely able to speak to listeners who shared my faith and love of country music. I was perfect for their market.

So I somehow managed to talk my way into the job. Of course, there was the challenge of convincing them to pay me a decent amount of money so that it would be a move up in the world, not a sacrifice, for my wife and children. Luckily for me, my old pal Paul Williams had been doing some consulting for Simmons on the side and whispered in the ear of the owners. It did the trick. He'd already smoothed the way for me, putting in a good word with Brian when he first came to Dallas, and now with the folks in Salt Lake. It was another key moment in my career where that man was my "Fairy Godfather."

Tears in a Parking Lot

The next hurdle was convincing Terresa. Even though I'd already mentioned I'd been chatting with folks in Salt Lake, I'd never said I was seriously interested in taking a job there. Better to wait until I had a solid offer than risk upsetting her for no reason, I figured. I broke the news when we were sitting in our car together, in a mall parking lot. She burst into tears. It was almost as if I'd told her I was having an affair and leaving her. At first, she couldn't understand why I'd want to tear our family away from the good life we'd built in Texas.

"But we have everything we could possibly want here!" she said. "Our beautiful house that we built together, our kids who love their school and their friends, *our* friends, my folks . . ."

She had a point. From the outside looking in, our life in Texas seemed ideal. I loved my colleagues like family and my in-laws like they were my own blood. We had scores of church friends, work friends, and friends we'd made through our kids' schools. And here I was ready to tear us away from this loving network of people and build a new one from scratch. Again, I felt I needed to choose the hard road. Starting over in a strange city with a young family is never easy. It was a risky move both on a personal and professional level.

The prospect was especially hard for Terresa because, aside from a brief spell living in Houston with her first husband, which was only forty-five minutes away by plane, she'd never lived far from her parents, friends, and extended family. I'd moved around the country from the time when I was a teenager, but here I was asking a home girl to move more than 1,200 miles away from everyone and everything she'd known her entire life.

"I'm so, so sorry!" I said as I put my arm around her and kissed her on her head, her face buried in my shoulder. "It's just that this is such a great career move for me. It's a chance for me to branch out on my own and be a kind of mini–Brian Philips, turning around a third-place station, leading a team, being a jack of all trades using all the skills I've learned here. It's something I've always wanted to try. I just need to do this."

Terresa finally stopped crying. Ever the supportive wife, she understood. She was always all about my career and happiness. Whatever it took to have that success, she accepted. She knew I was feeling stuck where I was, and that I had accomplished all I ever could at The Wolf.

"It'll be good for us, you'll see," I told her. "We'll be at the epicenter of our faith. We'll be able to attend church, go to the Salt Lake Temple, listen to the Mormon Tabernacle Choir, and really immerse ourselves in that life. We'll be surrounded by gorgeous mountains. We'll play in the snow. Maybe we'll even learn to ski. You've never experienced the place, and it is inspiring."

Breaking the news to her mom and dad was the worst part. There were more tears. They thought it was because of the

Mormon Church somehow making us go. I would not have put my wife and family through the move if I didn't believe it was the right step for my career and ability to provide for them. But by the way they reacted, it was as if they'd lost their little girl forever.

"I just know it's always going to be me who gets on the plane to visit them, and not the other way around," Terresa told me. "No one is going to come all that way to see us."

Bottle Brunette

When we got there, I was euphoric. The bracing new air and scenery, my fascination with building a brand at my very own station, along with the thrill of our total immersion experience in a Mormon town, were the perfect distractions. By then I'd taken enough career risks, following my instincts in ways that led to all kinds of success, that I tackled the new challenge with confidence. I knew I could be the badass with the killer resume who could swoop in and save the station. I was the king of my domain.

The kids were still young enough that they could adapt quickly to the transition. But for the first couple weeks, Terresa was miserable. Not that she complained. She always tried to make the best of things. But then one day I came home to a brunette.

It was Terresa's way of grieving for her old life. She was a natural blonde, with highlights from the sun that were almost platinum. That was her brand. Finding the darkest brown hair color on the drugstore shelf was her attempt at finding a new identity in a new town. I was a little surprised, because she didn't think to warn me, but she still looked stunning.

"Wow, it really makes the blue of your eyes pop!" I told her, doing my best to help her feel good about her decision.

We'd been invited to a school event that night. When some of the other parents saw the raven-haired beauty on my arm, a few of them feared I was stepping out on my wife. Or maybe I'd taken on a sister wife. Like I could handle more than one wife, in my situation!!

Terresa soon went back to being blonde. Not only had she made peace with her new situation, she had discovered a whole crew of old friends from the Mormon church in Dallas who'd moved to Salt Lake City. Suddenly she had a social circle and a purpose, involving herself in church and school activities while making our new house feel like home. Terresa started family traditions of our own, like Easter egg hunts and sledding parties. The neighboring dads would go out and build moguls on the hill by our kids' elementary school, to make it more interesting. When we'd had enough of crashing into the snow, we'd go to a neighbor's house for cider and hot chocolate, or the neighbors would come to ours (we took turns).

We went hiking in the mountains around Sundance Resort, and the kids took advantage of the free lift passes to learn how to ski. We visited haunted houses during Halloween. Oddly enough, Mormons are obsessed with Halloween. Gardner's Village, which was built in 1877, with its resident witches and corn mazes, is almost as popular as the temple, or at least as far as the kids were concerned. That first year in Salt Lake City was also the first time Terresa cooked the entire Thanksgiving dinner totally from scratch. She gathered up all her family recipes and made Texan cornbread in a Texas-shaped cast-iron skillet. It was delicious.

Tone Deaf

Terresa was happy and my kids were overjoyed. But that vision for myself of becoming a radio executive with a corner office at a successful station wasn't quite squaring with reality. My big ideas coming into a station and becoming a turnaround king like Brian soon got checked as I started navigating the personalities on the morning show I was coaching. Maybe I did have the winning formula, but I came on a little too strong. I was admittedly a bit cocky and brash back then, forcing my branding concepts down the throats of the old guard in a way that was causing indigestion. This fact was gently pointed out to me by one of the older executives at Simmons.

"Cody, there's only one way to boil a frog: slow. You've got to start with a low simmer before you gradually turn up the heat."

I never forgot those words, or the unfortunate image of a boiling frog. Eek! Listening to my "elder" helped me to correct course. I needed to start with a softer approach. I was so caught up in my own ideas that I wasn't fully listening to the people I was trying to help, learning their strengths, or finding ways to build the show around them. In my eagerness, I was tone deaf, and failed to read or, I should say, *hear* the room.

That's why Keith Stubbs, a local comedian who was the superstar of the morning show, was so resistant. Here I was, a young buck in my early thirties, trying to tell a man, who'd already built up a successful local following over the years, to suddenly change. It's not that he outright refused, but I could tell he didn't share my enthusiasm.

One of the issues was my carefully crafted branding strategy, to call our programming "Fresh Country." When I first came to Salt Lake City, what struck me was the fresh mountain air. Everything about the place was sparkling and crisp, from the snow-topped mountains to the gleaming faces of my fellow Mormons at the temple. There was a wholesome hopefulness about the community and Utah's big, wide-open landscape that I wanted to inject in all our music and imagery, to differentiate us from the old-school heritage stations we were competing against.

But Keith, as comics do, poked a little fun at the new approach.

"Here's your fresh flight of fresh country!" became, "Here's your FEEEERRRRRRRRRREEEESSHH flight of fresh countreee!!!!!!!!"

He threw his hands up at the line "Fresh Country Forecast" from the weather report.

"Do I really have to say that?"

He obliged, but I kept hearing that sarcastic comedian's inflection in his voice. It stung a little, but honestly, it was hilarious. Ultimately, he was right. Interestingly, we were both from South Carolina, we shared similar humble beginnings, and we were both Mormons. We also happened to be Type A and ambitious. Maybe that was why we clashed.

My gut told me Keith was thinking along the same lines I was. That perhaps I'd overstepped and needed to show appreciation for his talent, while encouraging us to work together as leaders on the station. One night, as I was driving home from the station's studios downtown, I took a chance and called him in hopes of a "come-to-Jesus" conversation.

"Keith, we have way too much in common not to enjoy this experience and work together to make the station the best it can be," I told him, as I was making my way down the steep hill in the snow toward our home in the Daybreak neighborhood.

"Yes, I can do that," he told me. "From now on, let's listen to each other and work *together*. I'm with you!"

I teared up as he said this. I was thrilled he felt this way, and relieved that the chat went so well.

Talk about a turnaround. From that point on, we got over our petty, stupid differences and have been the best of friends ever since. We started hanging out more, going to Brigham Young University football games together. Keith, who owned the Wise Guy comedy clubs in Salt Lake City, invited me to stand-up shows. Turns out we also shared a similar sense of humor. Maybe it's why I admit to laughing at his "Fresh Country" jokes.

Professionally, Keith began to understand that I wasn't trying to make him into something he wasn't. I had such high esteem for the man and his professional chops that, years later, I had him fill in for me at CMT. Even though I'd been the voice on the radio in Dallas, in this role I was happy to be the guy behind the scenes, helping his star to shine brighter and reach a broader audience. To that end, I hatched a scheme.

During the 2008 season of *American Idol*, a Salt Lake City home boy, David Archuleta, was one of the contestants. I decided that The Eagle would become the David Archuleta station. We would wrap ourselves around this fresh-faced kid, who looked like he actually had a shot at winning on what was then the hottest show on television. I called myself Cody Archuleta. When David sang a country song, we aired it. Every opportunity we could, we promoted him.

Of course, I was operating on a shoestring budget. I used to joke about how we ran the whole place with duct tape and barbed wire. But I figured there was nothing a bit of creativity and a lot of enthusiasm couldn't overcome. At that time, the movie *Napoleon Dynamite* was a favorite in the Mormon community, in part because there was an innocence to its stupid humor, and it was produced by and starred Mormons. Our friends were constantly quoting silly lines like, "Stay home and eat all the freakin' chips, Kip!" In one of the movie's scenes, a kid named Pedro runs for student council and has these T-shirts made up that say, "I Voted for Pedro."

I had hundreds of T-shirts made up in the same '70s font, with cheap-looking iron-on decal lettering that said, "I Voted for David Archuleta." We took our station truck to all the mall parking lots we could, giving these T-shirts away, and they became cool in a geeky kind of way. People latched on.

So, when David became a finalist on the show and came back home for a parade and concert, ours was the little radio station that Fox Television decided to film. They picked us over the much larger stations in the area, and we got our big prime-time TV moment. Our building was surrounded by hundreds of screaming tween girls as if David were one of the Beatles on *The Ed Sullivan Show.*

There was so much buzz about David, even among the Mormon church elders. They loved the fact that this wholesome-looking Mormon kid, one of their own, was getting millions of fans. One of these elders, who became another father figure of mine, asked me to bring David along to his box at a Utah Jazz basketball game to meet Thomas S. Monson, then president of the Church of Jesus Christ of Latter-day Saints, a huge deal for anyone of the Mormon faith.

Little did I know back then that David was facing similar struggles between his faith and his sexuality. In June 2021, he came out on Instagram as LGBTQIA+, describing himself as on the spectrum of bisexual, asexual, and "still in the process of trying to figure out what that means."

Since moving to Salt Lake, I'd met several senior clergy members of the church, but not the man who was considered to be the prophet. Accompanying David was my chance. We spent a good hour in conversation with President Monson, who asked me about my mission in Seattle and urged David to consider going on one himself. We talked about our faith, and what the church meant to us. It was an incredible moment. In a single day I felt I'd reached a professional and spiritual pinnacle. I can't even remember who won the game that night.

The *American Idol* moment served to raise Keith's profile, since he was the DJ who got to interview David, and his face aired all over the country. That was a good thing for The Eagle. But none of this effort translated into ratings for the station because our signal was too damn weak. I was working all hours and on weekends to make my mark, struggling to bring new voices and ideas to a station that simply did not have the tools or money to be heard. It was only reaching pockets of the Salt Lake City market. It doesn't matter how much you strive to make an impact when you don't have the frequency. You can have mediocre programming and still have success if you're operating on one hundred thousand watts versus just a few thousand. It was like serving up five-star food at a deserted roadside café. No one was there to taste it. As someone who was bursting with ambition, it was beyond frustrating.

Nashville Calling

Then Brian Philips, my former program director and mentor at The Wolf, called. He had since moved on to MTV and landed as their head of Country Music Television (CMT), which was launching a new show, *CMT Radio Live*. It would be a nationally syndicated show, and Brian wanted me to host it. I'd get to interview all the hitmakers of country. Was I still open to moving to Nashville, working for my old friend? *Well, hell yeah!* Or as they say in Utah, *Heck yeah!*

But I felt I'd barely begun in Salt Lake City. I'd only been at the job for a year and a half. My plan was to make it to the executive floor. Going back to being an on-air personality would be like taking a U-turn on the career path I'd mapped out for myself. I asked Terresa what she thought and, although she and the kids were finally loving their lives in Utah, she knew it was a dream job.

"We'll figure it out," she assured me. "We will go wherever you want to go and need to be."

It was a heartfelt struggle. The situation reminded me of the poem "The Road Not Taken" by Robert Frost: *Two roads diverged in a yellow wood, And sorry I could not travel both . . .*

The new job would require working nights, missing the family dinners, ball games, and ballet recitals. I would be building the program from scratch, with no infrastructure to speak of. There would be no time to even breathe; work would suck up all the oxygen. I canvassed the opinions of a few of my old friends and mentors in the industry, including Paul Williams.

"Yeah, you should probably take that job," he told me.

My agent, Paul Anderson, put it more bluntly.

"You'd be crazy not to take this job! This is a game changer. It's your chance to be the Ryan Seacrest of country radio."

It so happened he also represented Ryan Seacrest, so who was I to argue?

Of course, I'd always dreamt of hosting a country show in the town where most of the music was made. But the timing was never quite right. Maybe this time it was meant to be. Maybe there were certain things I had to go through first, risks I had to take, professional and personal growth I had to experience,

to be ready for this town that seemed more like the final destination than one of the many stops along the way. But was I
truly ready to make that leap to Nashville? At the very least, I
had to find out.

It was already becoming clear to me that I was never going
to be the perfect Mormon. Or the perfect anything except
maybe a country music host. My next road had to lead me to
the capital city of country music, where work and career would
become my religion. Again, it wasn't the easy path. For the first
year, while I tested the waters at CMT, I left my wife and children behind. I told myself I didn't want to risk once again pulling them away from their life at school and with friends, the
life they knew and loved, until I was sure.

End of the Line

As brief as it was, I'm glad we had that time as a family in Utah.
It gave all of us a chance to immerse ourselves in the Mormon
faith and take it as far as it could go. It gave my kids an opportunity to fully understand the religion they were being raised in
and take them to their spiritual roots. In some ways the experience helped us all to grow. No, the move didn't "fix" me, but
sometimes you have to take a road all the way to the end before
you can redraw the map of your life.

Once again, I found myself leaving behind a life that, from the
outside in, seemed ideal. In Salt Lake City I had faith, family, and
career all tied up in a bow. It was my last-ditch effort to get it
right. Instead of dialing into my inner, authentic self, I drowned
out that voice with the heavenly noise of church life. In the heart
of Mormonism, surrounded by a community that shared my
faith, I had hoped I could finally put an end to those urges.

I took listening to everything but my own voice as far as it could go. I tried tuning into God. Maybe He would speak to me and tell me what to do. Some religions have a Third Eye, but I think of hearing messages from your maker as more like having a Third Ear. When I allowed myself to be still enough, I would occasionally pick up on a few of those signs. But mostly the path I'd been on was a long, circuitous detour that only brought me back to myself, and at that point I wasn't ready to hear what "he" had to say. I'd reached the end of the line.

You can never drown out that inner voice, no matter how much you try. The harder and longer you try to shift the focus away from your true desires and your authentic self, the louder that voice in your head will eventually scream. Meanwhile, you'll live in denial and make all kinds of decisions that cut you off from the road to happiness. You may think you've got everyone fooled. But deep down they know something is missing and there's a breakdown in communication with the people you hold most dear. You're too busy just reacting to situations, listening to outside sources, and following your fears. You may not even know why you're unhappy. But there's always a reason.

I don't regret embracing my religion and doing whatever I could to hear God and do what I thought He was calling me to do. But that call from Brian was some other kind of divine intervention that pulled me off a path that, ultimately, was the wrong one for me.

Astronaut Dad

For months, I bounced between Nashville and Salt Lake City, a four-hour flight and a time zone away, two weekends a month and on holidays, when I did the broadcast from the basement of our family home. I worked in between two worlds and two states of mind, reasoning I needed to "settle in" to my new position and avoid disrupting the kids' school year.

I took full advantage of being miles away in a brand-new town to explore how it might feel to be single. It didn't take me long to fall in love with Nashville. I found plenty of entertainment and professional challenges to quiet the internal struggles I was facing. Nashville's story, and the characters who lived here, were the perfect distraction for a man who wanted nothing more than to escape himself. This wasn't necessarily a bad thing. It gave me the time and space I needed until I was completely ready to hear my own truth. Meanwhile, my external listening skills helped me to form fast friendships in a place where newbies had to work hard to earn trust.

I guess I always knew Nashville would be my forever home. I loved the concert halls, dive bars, and barbecue joints—places where you might find yourself sitting next to Blake Shelton drinking vodka and eating brisket. It's an industry town, and so much more, full of culture, surprises, beauty, and grit. It's a place that oozes authenticity, but more sophisticated than you might expect, equally wholesome, laid back, and family friendly—everything I love in a country song manifested in a place. Do I sound like I am getting paid by the local tourist board? I should be.

Unguarded

I quickly got comfortable in this new but familiar world, maybe a little too comfortable. I spent my "bachelor" weeknights meeting new friends, and on a few occasions ventured to meet other gay men, even though I wasn't yet ready to identify myself with that tribe. Sometimes on Grindr, the gay dating app, or even Craigslist, some new guy would catch my interest as I tried to decipher my feelings.

Nothing was happening. I only did it sporadically, cautiously dipping my toes in these waters. I didn't want to sleep with anyone, so these liaisons were just conversations, mild, verbal flirtations at most. Physically and emotionally, I'd never been with anyone else besides Terresa. I was trying to figure out if I even enjoyed conversations with a man before risking my livelihood or my family with this kind of disclosure.

Maybe it's all just a fantasy, I thought. *Something that's going to live inside my head and nowhere else.*

I felt like crud. Back in Salt Lake I was pretending to be someone else entirely, with my button-down shirts and pressed khaki pants, teaching classes on spirituality and going to church with my beautiful, perfectly dressed family, while I spent my evenings in Nashville as the contemporary, ballcap-wearing, energetic DJ thinking and almost acting upon things totally contrary to my belief system. There's always a sense of unworthiness in Mormonism, a religion that strives for perfection. In a sense, everyone is putting on a façade of devotion, faking it until they make it. But I felt like the biggest fraud of all. The dichotomy of my two lives was breaking me in half.

Act of Terror

Then the rumors started flying.

Paul Anderson, my longtime agent and friend, who also happens to be openly gay, called me out of the blue.

"Hey, I just heard from someone in radio who said you're running around in gay circles," he informed me.

"What?! Me? Of course not!" I told him, pretending to laugh it off.

It frightened the hell out of me. *I'd been discreet, hadn't I?* I must have underestimated my own visibility because, as a new-comer on the Nashville scene, it never occurred to me that I could be recognized. Maybe I didn't do enough to disguise my identity online. I certainly didn't think of myself as a celebrity. Paranoia took over my brain. *Who saw me, and why would they want to out me like that? If some random guy in radio knows, maybe others do too. Maybe the entire industry knows?!*

I felt shame and horror. Outing someone before they are ready, before they've had a chance to tell their loved ones and prepare themselves, can have devastating consequences. No one should be rushed into it. I needed to be ready.

Paying attention to your inner voice and hearing your own truth isn't necessarily like flicking a switch. It's a process. Some-times it's okay, even appropriate, to fully immerse yourself in another environment or aspect of your life until you are com-pletely ready to go there. Meanwhile, your focus on new people and places, flexing your listening skills to acclimate and get to know these new folks in your life, at least on a superficial basis, can serve you well to a degree.

I realized that eventually I would need to go deeper, but I wasn't ready for the big reveal as a gay man to myself, much less the world. *Hell,* I thought. *I've only just been singing hymns in a Mormon church with my wife and children! Hold on there!*

It was the first and only time I felt discriminated against as a gay man, and it shook me to my core. My agent wasn't being judgmental, he was just reporting what he'd heard from sources whose intentions were not necessarily kind. But he knew I had been presenting myself as a Christian family man in country music, and this was in 2009, before the US Supreme Court struck down state bans on same-sex marriage in 2015. This gossip was also going around only months after I landed the job at CMT, where I hadn't yet built the kind of reputation needed to withstand a scandal. Worse was the thought of my beloved wife and kids hearing the truth from any source other than me.

I guess Nashville is a smaller town than it looks.

((7))

THE CONVERSATION

And it's been a long time coming

Don't give up on me

I'm about to come alive.

—DAVID NAIL, "I'm About to Come Alive"

My contract at CMT said nothing about appearing on television. In fact, one of the first things Brian Philips asked me before I made the move to Nashville was whether I'd be okay with that.

"The TV folks are on one floor, and you'll be on another," he told me. "There may be some collaboration here and there, to promote each other's shows, but basically you're our radio guy."

It never occurred to me to put myself in front of the camera. I found out years later that Brian's reluctance was not because he viewed me as a "face made for radio." When he made his own transition to television, he'd been repeatedly told by MTV network executives to forget what he knew about our industry. Television broadcasting was all about casting pretty people in Hollywood to present the shows and interview the celebrities. When he made the decision to hire me, he told the network bosses, "No one should read too much into me hiring my friend Cody from my last station in Dallas. He'll be here to produce his own radio show and oversee *CMT Radio*, but in no way am I trying to impose him on our TV channel."

Brian felt bad about circumscribing my career in this way, so he asked our friend Paul Williams what he thought.

"Ah, no one wants to see Cody's bald head on television anyway!" Paul told him.

But apparently someone did. Within a couple of weeks of my landing in Nashville, CMT had put little notices up around the building about the launch of our radio show, to let internal staff know what was going on. This was their normal practice. If there was a new documentary or some other show of interest they wanted staff to know about, they plastered the news on these well-designed, 8 x 11–inch billboards in the lobby, in the elevators, in the lunchrooms. . . . John Hamlin, a senior producer for *60 Minutes*, who joined CMT as head of production, saw my picture and asked Brian if he could use me.

I guess he thought my face might not break the camera lens after all. There was also some awareness in the building that I knew how to pull off a great interview. All those years in Texas, speaking with callers, drawing them out and making them the star of the moment, had helped me raise my game as I led conversations with some of the top artists in the country music firmament.

At first, I appeared on some celebrity interview packages as "a reliable source." They were only brief segments, but I felt so comfortable and natural on air that I wanted more. They put me in that chair and the magic of the studio lights hit me hard. After doing radio for more than twenty years at that point, the taste of the new gave me an adrenaline rush.

Apparently, my enthusiasm translated well through the camera, because less than a year later, in 2010, I got my wish when I was asked to cohost a CMT show on the weekends called *#1 Music & a Movie*, with a redheaded and talented cohost, Alecia Davis. (Thank God for Alecia, who had a front-row seat to my sometimes awkward TV infancy.) Throughout the show, we'd share fun factoids about the movie and music that related to the film or the year it was released.

It was the perfect opportunity to grow into my new role as an on-camera personality, sitting at a desk with a microphone, reading from a teleprompter. The show was pre-taped, so there was a lot of patience and forgiveness and my confidence grew. This side gig combined my two loves: movies and music. It also provided me with a chance to ham it up and explore my inner camp.

Soon we were wearing crazy costumes to match the theme of the movie, or not. When we aired Mel Gibson's movie *The Patriot*, I dressed like one of our forefathers in colonial garb, including a powdered white wig. For *Blazing Saddles*, I went shirtless with a leather vest, with props and a green screen to make it appear as if I were riding a longhorn. *Mrs. Doubtfire* was my chance to do drag, with an enormous pair of strap-on boobs, a gray old-lady wig, beard, and bright red lipstick. For *Nacho Libre*, I dressed up as a wrestler with spiky blond Tina Turner hair, red and black tiger print spandex, and a cape.

The show caught on. Everyone wanted to know what the next ridiculous outfit would be. A chicken? A dog? Yes to both! I remember the show producers asking me if I'd feel comfortable donning a frog costume for a skit. I enthusiastically said, "Of course I will! I'm here to put on a show!" *This is what showbiz is!* I thought.

I should point out that my full-time television career didn't happen right away. It developed over my first couple of years at CMT, until I was made the permanent host of the newly rebooted version of *Top 20 Countdown*, called *Hot 20*, in January 2013.

The new TV show took off fast and has become CMT's flagship music show. A longtime producer for the great Larry King at CNN, Quinn Brown, was hired, and we hit it off right from the start, as he had an appreciation for radio-to-TV talent like Larry and me. Those months in Nashville, sampling television and traveling to shoot shows while building my own national radio show, made me giddy. I loved working those long hours and being in the mix of so many things I enjoyed.

I was also horny. *What would it be like if I could just live?* I wondered. Men were hooking up with each other late at night, a possibility that had never occurred to me. But my curiosity about the "gay world" got to me, and I started chatting with a few of them, asking what it was like for them to come out. I was hungry to hear other people's stories, yet it was the furthest thing from my mind to come out to Terresa. My true sexuality was something I'd only just begun to timidly explore. But I didn't connect the possibility of being outed with my increasing visibility through television until those rumors started. There was a flip side to all this added exposure. I was being forced to come out before I was ready.

Choking Out the Words

I knew I had to get ahead of this news or risk Terresa hearing something. But it was the conversation every closeted gay person dreads more than anything. Interviewing someone challenging on air was nothing compared to this most private of confessions. Saying those words, I mean actually getting them to come out of my mouth for the first time, was terrifying. You are practically choking as you give voice to the truth of who you are from deep inside. A lifetime habit of hiding is hard to break. I could barely admit this truth to myself. But if there was one person who deserved to know, it was Terresa.

I think sometimes she thought that my moods and emotional distance were because she had done something wrong. It wasn't her. I was being unfair. For her sake as well as mine, it was time. So, shortly after that close brush with a public outing, on a weekend visit back to Utah, after the kids were put to bed, I took a deep breath and told the one person in the world I trusted the most.

"There's something I need to tell you," I ventured. "But first I want you to know that you don't have to worry. I'm still here, and I'm not going to do anything about it."

Terresa gave me a confused look.

"I think I'm gay . . ."

She gasped. Then she looked me straight in the eyes and asked, "You think, or you know?"

"I've felt this way my whole life. I was never given a choice. But I want to try and figure this out, and I need your help."

I can't imagine what it felt like to hear those words from the man she loved more than anything. She'd never lost her desire for me, so to be told that I was turned on by dudes had to have hit her like a sucker punch to the gut. She did burst into tears. Hearing her sobs was heartbreaking, and I cried too. We held each other for the longest time, weeping together. But when she finally came up for air, I realized that her despair was not entirely about her own disappointment. My wife didn't blame me one bit. She never yelled or accused me of betrayal. At first, she wept not for herself, but for me.

"All these years you've been suffering in silence, alone! Why didn't I know, why didn't I guess? Was I just so self-obsessed that I haven't noticed what the person I love most in the world has been going through?"

I was floored. It never occurred to me that her first reaction would be a wave of grief and concern for my own pain. I'd always known that Terresa was the kind of woman who put others first, but this was another level of compassion and selflessness. She was angry at God, at society, at our church community, that I was ever made to feel that I should hide who I was from the world.

"Why couldn't I have seen you? Why couldn't I have helped you earlier? Am I so disjointed from the relationship that I couldn't see it?" she sobbed.

Terresa never blamed me for my moodiness.

"You went out of your way to make me feel loved and cared for," she told me. "We both had our moments when we needed our space, like any married couple. But never once did I imagine it was something deeper."

She had never had the slightest suspicion because I masked it so well. I also had the excuse of working long hours and feeling tired.

"Terresa, the fact that you never saw is not your fault! People are good at hiding this stuff, especially me."

I told my wife I loved her a million times, and I meant it. She was my person, and I was hers. But I couldn't fully love her the way a woman wants and deserves to be loved by a man. We were physical, clearly, because we had two beautiful children to prove it. But no matter how hard I tried, I knew I wasn't giving her all she deserved in a relationship. That shame I carried with me also, feeling that I had again fallen short as husband and partner. The romantic movie playing in my head was of me running into the arms of a man. That's what gave me butterflies.

Knowing this truth had to have hurt the woman in my life, despite her initial bravado and selflessness. Terresa kept a journal her entire life, but its last entry was March 21, 2009, the night of that first conversation.

"Some things I don't think I've dealt with," she told me recently. "I'm still working stuff out on a daily basis. But I never thought for one moment that you did me wrong."

Probing and Pausing

We had a series of conversations over the next few months . . . and years. Coming out was a gradual unfolding, as we both adjusted to the new reality. But I don't believe I could have done it without Terresa. Above all, she *listened*. Terresa wanted nothing more than to hear my truth and completely understand the man she had married, without judgment. There was absolutely no blame on her end. Instead, she promised to stand by me, and assured me that I was a good father and a good man.

By asking probing questions, pausing for answers, and paraphrasing my words back to me in a sincere effort to understand, she helped me to clarify my own true desires. By hearing what I had to say with pure, selfless love, she helped me dial into my inner voice.

In one frank discussion we were having in the kitchen, when I shared more about my feelings for men and what it felt like to live in my skin, Terresa made it clear she understood I was born this way.

"I don't believe you chose this," she told me. "I don't believe you would make this up, because why would you put yourself through all this pain?"

I was still struggling. Feeling gay and acting upon it are two completely different things, and I wasn't sure I could ever go there. Of course, I needed to find out.

"Well, you're not going to know until you know," she said.

And from that comment I knew that Terresa is the strongest, most compassionate person I've ever met. I adore her, and always will.

Make no mistake, it was far from a smooth transition to where we are now. There were many moments of hurt and anger, but we always came back to that place of compassion for each other. In 2010, when it was obvious that the Nashville gig would work out and I could move my family, I flew back to Salt Lake City for the weekend and took Terresa out on a "date" to our local Olive Garden to discuss next steps. Yes, Olive Garden! Love those endless breadsticks! I mean, who doesn't?

"If you want to go back home to Dallas, if that's where you need to be, I can set you up in a house there," I told her. It was my attempt to return her to what I believed was her happiest setting. I also thought, *At some point, she'll dump me.* And in part, my offer was to prepare her and me for that eventuality.

"Why Texas? You are in Nashville, and you are the father of my children," she said.

"But you don't know anyone there, and I work long, late hours. I can fly fast to Dallas. I've been doing it for the past year and a half. Even in my condition."

"Yes, *our* condition," she said. "We're still a family. We go where you go, no matter what."

One Last Shot

It was at that point I decided to recommit to our marriage. When I moved Terresa and the kids to Franklin, an upper-class, gorgeous suburb just outside of Nashville, I figured I'd go back to being the family man. We found a house near the local Mormon church. We got Landon and Makayla enrolled in a great school close by. My sexuality would remain something private, between Terresa and myself, that we put in a box and set aside to see if we could give this conventional family life one last shot.

We fasted and prayed together. I waded through books and online documentation about dealing with homosexuality inside the faith. I wanted to understand why people turned out to be gay. Was it circumstances, or was I just born this way? I read *The Miracle of Forgiveness* by Spencer Kimball, a past president of the Mormon Church, which basically said that I had to strive to overcome my "sins." The whole book wallowed in the concept of shame. It was one heart-wrenching read. I also read *In Quiet Desperation: Understanding the Challenge of Same-Gender Attraction*, coauthored by Ty Mansfield, a married Mormon who was into men. He concluded that no man could love him as much as Jesus does.

During one of my most fervent prayers, I asked God to take this burden of being gay away from me.

"Lord, help me know what I should do! Help me to know if I need to stay on this path as Terresa's husband!"

Deafening Silence

But I got nothing. As hard as I tried to listen, He wasn't talking. It was more of a one-sided conversation. I had guilt-based dreams that I tied back to an answer, but all they did was muddy my thoughts. In one of our Mormon classes, I raised my hand in frustration.

"I get that God works in mysterious ways, but does He have to be this subtle?" I asked. "If He's really there, why doesn't He answer life's big questions?"

I'd been doing my part: I paid the church tithings, abstained from alcohol, obeyed every little rule of our community. What was with the silence?

My bifurcated existence in Nashville was becoming even more of a struggle, Sundays especially. It was the one day I couldn't escape myself at work, when I had to go through the motions of attending a church that no longer uplifted me. I was also beginning to suffocate in my marriage, as loving and understanding as Terresa was being. I took an apartment downtown, on the excuse that I was working crazy hours, especially on award show nights. It was a way of separating church and state, although I still felt plenty of guilt as I went back and forth between single guy in the city and suburban family guy.

At times, my life looked like that movie *I Am Michael* with James Franco, the true-life story of a guy named Michael Glatze, who gave up his homosexuality to become a Christian pastor. He believed God didn't love him because he was gay, so he forced himself to be straight until he fell in love with the next man who paid attention to him. Mormonism, like many religions, doesn't accept homosexuals as members of their church unless they are willing to take a vow of chastity and never practice gay sex. That's exactly what I tried to do until I realized there was no praying the gay away.

Between Two Worlds

Eventually, I turned to a therapist. He explained how sexuality is not black and white, but varying shades of gray, and that feelings of love and sexual excitement exist on a spectrum.

"Eventually, being who you are will not be a detriment to your life," he assured me.

That was a turning point. After years of carrying around guilt and shame about who I was on the inside, I finally understood I was born this way, and that all the church stuff I'd been reading about homosexuality was, as my mother would say, hogwash. I started blossoming. It was at that point I fully understood my being gay was a fact I was never going to change. I'd been living in two worlds and never felt complete in either one of them. It was time to choose the one that was meant for me.

I'd always strived to be a man of integrity, but during that period especially, it struck me that I was falling short in this regard because I had spent a lifetime masking who I was at my core. I was twisting myself into knots to live right according to the Bible, but denying my sexuality was lying by omission. If honesty was among the highest ideals, how could I possibly attain it by hiding?

Terresa didn't take the news of my wanting to separate well. She was afraid of being left alone. This was the price of not ripping the Band-Aid clean off our marriage. I had unintentionally lulled her into thinking that our family would always look like the Romneys or something out of a 1950s sitcom, apart from the fact that Dad liked dudes. There was a big fight leading up to the time I made the move out of the house more official, one of the few times Terresa showed any real anger or frustration with me.

"But what would you have me do?" I finally asked her. "You've got to believe that, as much as I love you, there is nothing I can do to change this. I've got to be me!"

"Yeah, I know. You've got to embrace this," she told me. "I'm heartbroken, but at the same time I know you'll always be there for me. You'll never do me wrong. We'll always be family, but who says it has to look a certain way? It's better than forcing you to keep living a lie."

We agreed to put off the divorce and telling the kids until they were "mature" enough to handle it. For now, this knowledge of who I was would stay between me, Terresa, and a small, trusted circle of my closest friends. What mattered was that we'd finally reached an acceptance about what needed to be.

Quiet Assurance

Garth Brooks's song "Unanswered Prayers" has some lines in it that resonate with me:

> Remember when you're talkin' to the man upstairs
> That just because he doesn't answer doesn't mean he don't
> care . . .

The song is about a guy who bumps into his old high school sweetheart while he's at a hometown football game. He's with his wife as he stares at the woman from the past, remembering the time he asked God to "make her mine." Then he realizes God didn't answer that prayer, because it would have made him miserable. The girl he loved in high school wasn't the angel he thought she was. God knew better.

I had asked God to change what could not be changed and believed He either could not, or would not, hear me. But all along He was quietly allowing me to come into my own truth. The answer didn't come in a flash or an epiphany. It wasn't like the scenes I'd imagined when I was a little kid listening to my mother describe the rapture. The voice of God wasn't booming, deep, or resonant as in Morgan Freeman's portrayals. It was more like a knowing or feeling that strengthened my resolve. It was a gradual realization that I was still the same good person growing up, serving on a mission, caring for my family. I *was* righteous and worthy. By virtue of digging within and hearing that voice, I was able to wipe away all the past shame and draw closer to God. That was His way of speaking to me. We tend to put our human expectations on what we want God to be. But my way of finding peace was to let go of those expectations and just be.

Until that moment of self-acceptance, I'd been determined to play certain roles to perfection. From the time I was a child in South Carolina, listening to Rick Dees's Weekly Top 40 countdown, I've known what I wanted to do. I built my career from small-town southern boy to one of country music's most influential radio and television personalities, visualizing and then living the dream with a single-minded determination to succeed.

I played the movie in my head, imagining the person I wanted to become, and then became him, first through my pretend broadcasts on Mr. Microphone, and then filling in on a late-night shift at my local radio station when I was fifteen. It all led me here, to a level of success way beyond anything I could have imagined when I was deejaying my high school dance parties and dressing up as my local radio station's mascot, Opie the Possum. And there'd been so many costumes since.

I've always played that movie in my head, hearing and visualizing the dream and imagining it as if it were already happening.

I played the family movie and got the perfect wife and kids.

I played the church movie and threw myself into my faith, becoming the model of a Mormon family man.

I was constantly rehearsing in my head what I might say, and how things would land, and for years that made me deaf to some potentially joyful and enriching experiences and interactions with others. I imagined how I thought I wanted my life to look, sound, feel, and be, and I got it. But the one movie I didn't dare to play was of my life as a gay man. I couldn't imagine myself in a fulfilling romantic partnership. For me there was no running movie of that final piece of the happiness puzzle, the true love you hear about in country songs.

Compassionate Listener

I had everything—a thriving career, a beautiful family, standing in my community and my church—and I never felt more alone. Denying myself that one true love created a void in my life I could no longer ignore. I needed to become totally honest with myself and the person closest to me, my wife, Terresa. Together, we slowly and carefully unraveled our marriage, praying to God to show us the right path forward. It was a long and delicate process. But listening with compassion to my wife, who in turn heard me out with patience and loving-kindness, got us through, and I'm proud to say the bond I share with Terresa and my kids is stronger than ever to this day.

I don't believe I could have come out the other side of this without Terresa's unwavering love and understanding. She opened the door and gave me the courage to recognize and embrace my authentic self. Creating a safe space, encouraging me to spit it out, then hearing all I had to say on a difficult subject with understanding, was an act of compassionate listening. It was also an act of emotional courage. Lord knows it could not have been easy for her to hear my truth. Yet she made it much easier for me with the gentle tone of her voice, the openness of her body language, the love in her eyes, and the instinctive way she knew when to be silent and let me talk. I can't imagine what my life would be like now if Terresa had changed the subject or shut me down. But she didn't.

She rode the roller coaster of pain and confusion right alongside me, and I still carry a lot of guilt about that. But today she appreciates me for being real with her. Her main concern was my happiness and, even though it hurt, she knew the situation at home was never going to get better if I was always pretending. She let me be me, and our relationship has never been healthier or happier.

The Subtle Voice

Getting to that last layer of the onion has also been a spiritual journey. I am okay with God now. To me, God is no longer relegated to being a bearded man in a white robe who makes up rules for human souls. Rather, I've seen that God is much bigger than that, more concerned with connection to my own soul and showing kindness to the world and love to those around me. I do hear and feel that same presence of Spirit, even as a gay man. I can hear God in the stillness of my mind, when I take in a deep breath, exhale, and allow the quiet assurance of that inner voice. It's much simpler than the process of looking so hard for signs that you miss them altogether. God's answer is

often the feeling of certainty and calm I receive about a particular path I am taking. It's the trust I now have in my own best
instincts.

I ultimately decided to leave a church that would not accept
me fully as a gay man. I refused to believe my Creator would
make me this way just to suffer. Leaving the Mormon community was painful, and I am still working through aspects of that
loss. I still maintain good friendships with Mormons who accept me now, some even hoping the church would change
enough to embrace those of us who are different. But for me to
change who I am to fit into some mold is not what God wants
for me. Instead, I've realized that those I care about love me for
me, and that I am a good, God-loving person regardless of what
the rest of the world thinks. This ability to live an authentic life
free of the inner turmoil of the past has been God's greatest gift
to me.

• FROM EVERY ANGLE •

by Landon, Cody's son

A TIME-OUT AT THE AGE of five is one of my earliest memories. Dad and Mom sat me down on the bottom of the stairs for thirty minutes in our house in Texas. I can't recall what I'd done exactly, but the reason that episode sticks out so much is that it's the only time I was ever really punished. Growing up, I was never grounded. I was just a regular kid, but I never got into any trouble at that level. Instead, if there was a problem, we'd just talk it out. Dad is a big communicator. Whatever decision I had to make or issue I was struggling with, he would come at it from every possible angle. But he also listened and let me talk.

I'm not saying he's the kind of fun dad who just wants to be my friend. He's all that and more, but there was always a sense of parental guidance. I respected his authority, but never once did I feel I had to hide a thing from my father. He knows everything about me. I think those conversations are what led me to make better decisions. We had one of those talks when I announced I wanted to move out of my mom's house in the middle of the pandemic. Dad disagreed. He felt that, at eighteen, I was too young. Besides, I had all the support and convenience I needed at home, which is close by the music school I was attending. Financially, staying home would also enable me to save money. He was right, of course. But I wanted to experience the whole moving out thing. I wanted to be free. We came up with a compromise that gave me the sense of independence I craved, with a kind of safety net.

As busy as his career has been, Dad's always made the time, and I'm probably closer to him than to anybody. I share his passion and drive, as well as his ear for music. The one difference is that Dad's a social guy and I'm an introvert, although I can turn it on if I have to. Knowing this, he checks in without being intrusive, dialing into my frequency and never forcing me to share if I'm not ready. Instead, we do stuff together, just the two of us, like go-carting or bowling when we first moved to Nashville, going to the movies, and grabbing a Five Guys burger afterward.

We did bowling and burgers before the big talk, when he came out to me. We went back to his apartment, he sat me down on the couch, and he told me everything. I was only fourteen, but he didn't dumb it down. He was just honest. I probably suspected by then, but at first it felt weird to hear it out loud, because I'd never met any gay people before. But the one thing I knew was that nothing would change between us. Looking back, it was pretty awesome that we had that conversation.

I'm so happy with the big and very different family we have now. I love my family, and I love my dad. I never thought this would be the way my life would go, but I'm glad it did.

• A DOTING DAD, PART 2 •

by Makayla, Cody's daughter

HI, IT'S ME AGAIN. I just want to say that, while there isn't a thing about my past life I would ever change, this version of my family is the one I love the most. Today, we are the happiest we have ever been. Dad 2.0, the man who embraced who he is, is one of my best friends. We can be goofy together. The other day we went shopping, and he decided to buy us matching full-length coats. We spent the next four hours wearing these jackets with sunglasses, setting up our phones for selfies in random corners of the mall.

We check in with each other daily. If I don't hear from him, I'll call him, worried something is wrong. There are no secrets because he is a stickler about keeping the lines of communication open. Too much of a stickler sometimes. Sometimes we'll be driving somewhere, and he'll demand to know what I'm thinking in that moment. If something's going on, he'll drag it out of me one way or another.

I'm not saying he's the perfect listener. He has "selective dad hearing" sometimes. If I ask him to name three of my friends, he might be able to name one. But if it's important, he zeroes right in. And he lets me do the same for him. I love the fact that he leans on me as an adult as much as I lean on him.

The best part of this new version of our family is how we've expanded. Trea is my bestie. We go out to bars together, with Dad, my mom, and her boyfriend. I've told both of my parents that if they ever break up with their boyfriends that's just too bad, because they're going to be in my life no matter what.

Sometimes we have a little too much fun together, like the time Trea, two friends of ours, and I got tipsy and rented some scooters to go to CMA Fest. Trea hit a speed bump and went flying, then his friend went over, then my friend skidded onto the human pileup. We laughed so hard, then went on to the concert. Trea had such a great time that he didn't notice he'd fractured his wrist until the next morning. I haven't been on a scooter since.

((**8**))

TUNED IN

Sometimes you want to throw the towel in
But you come out swinging like you just might win.
—JACK INGRAM, "Keep On Keepin' On"

C arrie Underwood was nervous. It was 2005, and we were in New York City, where, for the first time, the Country Music Awards were to be broadcast out of the Big Apple. Carrie was to be my first interview for the CMA special I was taping for The Wolf. Fresh off her win on *American Idol*, we all knew she was going to be a huge star. Simon Cowell is not exactly one of country music's biggest advocates, but from the minute she walked on that stage and auditioned for him, it was obvious. The fact that he predicted her success was a huge deal at the time. But America's sweetheart was a simple girl. You might even call her green, and nowhere near as skilled and polished at this media game as she became after more than fifteen years of practice.

Sensing she was uncomfortable from her body language and those big, caught-in-the-headlights doe eyes of hers, I grabbed a gadget called an iDog from the desk. This was back in the early days of iPods and iTunes, when stuff like this was a novelty. The thing would light up, play music, and dance to its rhythm. We were having fun, laughing and playing around with this stupid robot dog when, suddenly, Carrie relaxed, the conversation started flowing, and I pressed the *record* button.

In those situations, when it's clear the person I am interviewing is preoccupied, tense, or simply having an off day, I never try to force things. Instead, I use my listening skills to dial into how someone is feeling and respond accordingly. All it takes is a little awareness and empathy to shift the mood. It no longer felt like an interview, just a goofy moment as two friends sat down and got to know each other a little better.

Listening doesn't just involve using one of your senses. You need all five to read the energy, body language, mood, and boundaries of the person you are with. To really be able to connect and build trust that can lead to an honest conversation, you have to put yourself in the other person's shoes and understand how they are feeling in that moment. Know what you would want to hear, and how you would like to hear it, then package your message accordingly. Whoever you are sitting or standing across from, all it takes to have a great conversation is the right mixture of empathy and humility. As a matter of fact, that should be the first rule of any interview.

I've gotten much better at bringing out the best in my radio and television guests over the years. But the two things I've always tried to do when I'm interviewing someone is make them comfortable and allow them to talk. This interview aspect of the job is about shining the light on them, not talking about myself, unless sharing a little personal information or banter is called for as an icebreaker. When I am open and authentic with people, they usually return the favor.

I'm always prepared with my questions, but I never interrogate, and if they want to take the conversation in another direction, so be it. I am always careful not to be so busy rehearsing what I want to say in my head, or listening for the sole purpose of responding, that I fail to catch the full meaning of what's being communicated. It's what many call being "present." I pay attention to what they are saying and let the mood and flow of the story guide me to places that often end up being more interesting than the Q&A I prepared for them the night before. It's a balancing act of spontaneity and careful guidance through a loose set of talking points to make sure we stay somewhat on track and give their fans the information they want to hear.

Here's Johnny!

One of my role models for this approach was Johnny Carson. I already mentioned how, growing up, if I could stay awake late enough, I'd watch his show and take in the subtle ways he made his guests shine when they took that seat next to his desk. It didn't matter if they were the little kid a producer found for the show who could do bird impersonations, a random oddball, or the biggest celebrity of the day, like Burt Reynolds, Johnny would make them the star, speaking and asking questions for the sole purpose of getting them to say something interesting or create the perfect setup to allow them to be their witty and best selves. A case in point was Charo, a comedienne and flamenco guitarist who would go berserk, running up and down the aisles, screaming, "Cuchi, cuchi!" at the audience members.

Johnny didn't mind that it took the attention away from him, or that it broke all the talk show rules, because he knew it made for great television. Unless it was for the sake of a self-deprecating moment to make his audience laugh, his success came from a quiet graciousness that put others in the best possible spotlight. He was a master of listening for that perfect opening to make his guest funnier, smarter, and more interesting than they ever thought they could be.

I try to emulate his kindness as an interviewer. I never ask gotcha questions, but I pride myself on getting more out of the country stars I interview than most. There is a certain rhythm to it. Through the cover of an album or tour they want to promote, taking a line from a song, or playing a word game, I can get them to spill before they even know what's happening, and they're happy to do it, because it comes out in a way that's light-hearted and relevant.

It's a subtle skill set, but it's well worth honing even if you aren't a media host, because listening, watching, and paying attention to the mood in the room while being open and curious about others will serve you well as you deepen your relationships with other people. Since that early interview with Carrie, we've become personal friends. One of the first major country artists to come out and publicly support gay marriage, Carrie was thrilled when I told her I met the love of my life while covering one of her concerts in Atlanta. And to think it all started with the simple kindness of letting her play with that dancing dog!

Keeping ears and minds open reaps some unexpected rewards because you never know who is listening. The fact that I give my guests the respect they deserve, researching their careers so that I can ask just the right questions to put them at ease and set up a humorous or thought-provoking response, has helped me build street cred in Nashville and beyond. Recently, Gayle King sent me a direct message, letting me know she was watching my show and has become a regular viewer. That was a welcome surprise that gave me goose bumps. Move over, Oprah—I'm Gayle's new best friend!

Sending and Receiving

My best interviews have taught me that good listening is about being able to receive and interpret messages with accuracy. It requires focus. Whether someone is speaking or singing to you, whether you are a passive listener or you are involved in a two-way conversation, treat what the other person has to say like a great country song. Put away the phone, cut past whatever minor distractions are going on around you, and tune out the monologue running in your head. Listen for those meaningful pauses, the tone, and the emotions behind the words. Put your focus entirely on the person speaking. Not only will you be enriched by the information coming your way, you will earn the trust and respect of the folks who matter most to you when you give them the gift of your time and attention.

Of course, staying focused on the person in front of us is even more challenging with our iPhones constantly pinging. Distractions have never been greater, with the constant onslaught of social media, Twitter and Instagram, and the never-ending list of cable, satellite, and streaming channels. In my business, if you don't make yourself worthy of your audience's time and focus with content that's compelling, you might as well be roping the wind.

That's why I can't allow myself to be as distracted as the average listener. Paying attention and being enough in the moment to see what's going on with others helps me to twist, pivot, and adapt as each situation requires. It enables me to show up and be fully on. The better you are at hearing what others have to say, the sharper your observations will be, so that you can cut through the clutter.

Barrel Boy

In my world, there are multiple things going on in any given moment beyond social media, and no day is exactly the same. When I'm in Nashville, my day starts with what we call "prep." I turn on the computer, blast the radio, and read through all the press releases gathered together by my producers, looking and listening out for the pop culture news of the day: pertinent country music info like the release of Thomas Rhett's new album, or stories paying tribute to the late, great Charley Pride. This is what we call "Hot Headlines with Cody," which we record, edit, and play several times a day.

I'm a restless guy who will always change things up just for the sake of variety. It keeps me fully engaged. Every day brings a different, joyful moment. I could be in the studio with Blake Shelton, who's joking about my Chuck Taylor Converse sneakers ("Man, who are you going to trust in the exit row—me in my cowboy boots or some guy in clown shoes?"); or covering a festival in Indiana, drinking rum with Kenny Chesney in his traveling tiki bar; or on the road in Texas, sitting behind Miranda Lambert's retro Airstream drinking Randaritas (Crystal Light, lemon lime soda, ice, and "good" vodka); or doing a live

CMT television broadcast outside a stadium in Phoenix, trying to focus while the KNIX radio mascot, "Barrel Boy," a fat dude wearing nothing but a beer keg with cowboy boots, dances around and does his best to distract me.

If you were to accurately list my job description, it would go on for pages, and all of the above would be just a few of my favorite things. Another one is a show called *Crossroads*, where, every couple of months, hot music acts get together with artists from other genres to sing each other's songs. Recently we did this with Florida Georgia Line and the Backstreet Boys. It's a segment that's rich in powerful music moments.

Another one of the joys of my ever-changing job is visiting the US military bases across the country and around the world. In June 2020, we joined the American Forces Network, which beams my radio show into more than one thousand bases globally, as well as more than two hundred ships at sea. Just a handful of shows have the honor of being on that network. They are picky about who goes on their airwaves—only the best for our military. But even before that, we built a special relationship with our armed forces. I've taken our broadcasts on the road and over the bases from Arizona to Alaska, South Korea to Bahrain. We always bring music acts to perform for the enlisted men and women, and it went so well that first time, the bosses at CMT said, "Let's do this every year!"

Army Insider

In 2019, during Thanksgiving week, our last in-person trip before the world changed, we joined Craig Morgan on his twelfth USO tour to Camp Humphreys, about an hour outside Seoul,

South Korea. The place was huge, like a city unto itself. Craig had spent more than ten years of his life on active duty in the US Army in the 101st and 82nd Airborne Divisions, and another six and a half years in the Army Reserves, so it was pretty cool to show up with an Army insider. We also brought along four Dallas Cowboy cheerleaders to bring some seasonal cheer. We took in some of downtown Seoul, an intensely crowded place full of markets, temples, and stores. I found it interesting to see how many people wore masks, little knowing how much masks would become such a major part of our consciousness just three months later. When we got back to the base, I did the *Hot 20 Countdown*, and Craig gave a concert inside the Collier Community Fitness Center, which had oceans of space that filled up fast with soldiers.

One of the best parts of the visit was meeting the commanders and active-duty men and women at the Spartan Dining Facility, the Super Hangar, and the Sentry Village USO. It was my chance to walk around with our producers and be accessible to our regular listeners in the military, people on the ground who are serving our nation. We struck up casual conversations with people, hoping we'd find a great story to share with our listeners, something that would help promote life in the armed forces. We met a young lady, a gunnery sergeant who told us her mom watched our show religiously.

"Can we FaceTime her?" I asked, ever the opportunist.

"Sure!" she answered, beaming a megawatt smile.

Although it was a bright and crisp winter's day in Korea, it was the middle of the night back where her mother lived, but she didn't mind, and called home while our cameras were rolling.

"You've got the best soldier right there!" her mom said.

Sticky Moments

This job allows me to immerse myself in those moments. I pretty much need to be switched on and completely engaged, since, as you've just read, there is no single typical day for a country music TV and radio host, at least not this one. Because so much is competing for my attention and can go south on a dime, I need to be able to regroup immediately, so that what the audience sees and hears is seamless.

Some of the chaos is self-induced, because I never like to sit still. I'll mix up the playlists or the run of the show to make it exciting and new. I reinvent because I am uncomfortable with comfort. I need to be challenged, so I'm always tinkering to keep things fresh. I also like to change up my environment. I love to be out there, catching those raw and real experiences backstage and on the road with artists; before COVID-19 put our world on pause, I was racking up the air miles. When I wasn't in the studio, I was zigzagging across the country, making sure I was at every music festival, and parachuting in at least once on every major artist's concert tour. In the summer especially, I could spend half the month on the road because I want to bring my listeners and viewers a unique experience. By the time you read this, I pray we can all be out there again, enjoying country music as a live audience as God meant us to do.

Keith Urban once told me, "You make Ryan Seacrest look like a slacker." I wouldn't go that far, but I sure do love him for saying it. Like Ryan, I do my homework. When I have an interview, which is most days, my producers and I will do some research and prepare a list of questions. My team is especially good at digging up interesting factoids and helping me come up with an angle that will not only get to the album or song the artist is promoting (that's usually why they're there), but create a moment that I call "sticky," something human and memorable that people will talk about, and that we can dine out on for days or even weeks. For that moment to be truly adhesive, it's not necessary that you remember exactly what was said, but you always remember how it felt.

These nuggets can't be forced. They are the rewards of tuning into someone's frequency. It's not as if I can engineer them ahead of time through my list of questions. They happen when someone starts to go down an unexpected path. Instead of rushing onto the next question, I let the conversation unfold, pausing to keep the interview subject talking or allowing them the time to think about a question and respond in a way that's heartfelt and authentic, then gently guiding them in the right direction. Dingo, who I brought with me from The Wolf when I first joined CMT, can always tell when I've picked up on something in the conversation that might be juicy.

"You look like a golden retriever who's happily wagging his tail when he suddenly hears something no one else does," Dingo once told me—his way of paying me a compliment. "Suddenly your eyes brighten, your ears perk up, and you sit up extra straight. That's when we know it's going to be good."

An example of a sticky moment includes my interview with Paula Deen in 2013 (before her N-word controversy). As a fellow southerner who loves to eat her stick-to-your-ribs dishes, we naturally hit it off. We could chat about Crock-Pot recipes for days. I knew Paula was a little out of her element during the interview because she wasn't in the kitchen, so I asked her a random question to warm her up:

"What's your favorite thing to cook?"

"Potatoes! Think about it. You can boil 'em, mash 'em, fry 'em, bake 'em, scallop 'em. I don't give a crap, honey. Just give me a potato!"

That little throwaway moment got played on tons of show breaks afterward. But the real story happened after the interview, during a photo shoot, when she pinched my butt! It became a part of my schtick for months after the interview ran.

"Can you believe that Paula Deen pinched my butt?" I'd randomly ask.

Another gem was when Dog the Bounty Hunter stopped by the studio. Weirdly, I've been a fan of his show, which also ran on the CMT network, and set my DVR to record it for years. But what I didn't realize was that Dog was also a fan of *my* show. His late wife, Beth, a sweetheart, told me how he watched the countdown every weekend, trying to guess what the top song would be.

"Who'd have thought that you, a metro hipster, would hit it off so well with a mullet-wearing guy who chases down criminals and did time in a Texas state penitentiary," said Dingo.

Dog was likable and disarmingly humble. And it just goes to show how it doesn't matter who you are or what your background is. Country music is the great uniter!

I pride myself on being able to get someone to reveal something about themselves that no one else can. It doesn't have to be something huge; it just has to help listeners to relate to a celebrity as a human being. To that end, I craft questions they aren't likely to expect. Like the time I asked George Strait if he is ever on Twitter. "Nope," he told me. "I don't tweet. I twang!"

Or when I asked Kenny Chesney if he cried when Bubba died in the movie *Forest Gump*.

"Yeah, I was on a first date," he started to tell me, then paused. "I don't think I told anyone this before, but the fact was, she didn't cry, so I broke up with her!"

Kenny's done thousands of interviews over the years, so I took the fact that he shared something with me that he'd never spoken of before as a huge compliment.

A Gentle Prod

Some interviews require an extra level of sensitivity. There might be something going on with a celebrity's personal life that's been made public, and I need to broach with them, because their fans will want to know. But, having lived with fear of exposure for most of my adult life, I understand that there is a right way and a wrong way to bring up a sensitive subject. I never go for the direct attack. I couch the question in language that's broad enough to allow them to gracefully dodge or answer in a vague way so that we all know what they mean, but we can leave it at that. Why poke when you can gently prod and cause less discomfort?

This was the approach I took when I interviewed the Queen of Country, Reba McEntire, after she announced that she was getting divorced. I referenced the news, then talked about how many of my listeners are going through divorce, or some other huge life change, and made it more about my audience by asking, "What advice do you have to give to anybody going through an evolution in their life or relationships?"

She answered candidly, admitting that the divorce was not her idea, and it hit her hard. But then she talked about how she wanted everyone in her life to be happy, and that life was too short for another person to be miserable in a relationship.

"So I just thought it was the best thing to take my marbles and go play somewhere else, like what my daddy used to always say."

It was a surprisingly philosophical and sticky quote that people would remember for a long time to come. It was also a healing moment because it enabled Reba to use what she was going through to help others. She added that she was getting through it by praying to God to help her put one foot in front of the other and fulfill her purpose on this earth, and surrounding herself with great girlfriends, family members, and people in her squad who loved her.

Never be afraid to lose yourself a little in the other person. Show up for them; let them see in your face that you're completely with them in the present moment, because you'll never get another quite like it. Of the more than 3,600 interviews I've done over the years, it's hard to pick a favorite, but I loved the time I spent with NASCAR champion Dale "The Intimidator" Earnhardt Senior while I was still at The Wolf, shortly before his life came to a tragic end in February 2001, when his car crashed in the last lap of the Daytona 500. I feel blessed to have had that precious time with him. I shared my feelings with his son Dale Junior when I interviewed him just shy of his fortieth birthday for CMT. He spoke to me about how fleeting life is.

"I can't believe where the time's gone really—to be honest with you," he told me. "It felt like just the other day I was twenty-six years old and just getting going and starting my career. I look back and I remember all the things that we accomplished and all the years that we were racing and the things that we went through."

It was another human-to-human, full-circle moment in the booth where the circumstances momentarily melted away and I could lose myself in the conversation.

The F-Bomb

Again, those authentic moments are all about getting the person I am interviewing off script and out of his or her own head. One trick I occasionally use to keep things real is to drop an F-bomb off the air right at the beginning of a conversation. I'll say something like, "What a f*&#ing awful 2020." I'm not generally a cusser, but it's my way of letting a bit of air out of the tire if there's some tension in the room. I'll also research random facts to see if I can come up with a curveball question. When we're preparing for a show, we'll do a wide sweep of whatever information is out there, from Facebook to Twitter to stories on the celebrity news sites, the more out of left field the better.

"Put that in the Crock-Pot and let it simmer," I tell my team, meaning the best ideas aren't always ready until they've had a chance to marinate, although Dingo once shot back: "But that's where some of my best ideas go to die!"

Not always. One juicy morsel that floated to the top of a Jason Aldean pop-up interview was a tweet his wife made about the fact that he doesn't like to have his bare feet touch the floor. I brought it up right at the beginning of the interview.

"I grew up with carpeting, but now we have a distressed hardwood floor, which is rough on my feet," he told me.

"Oh yeah?"

"I could be a foot model with these things."

I told him I was glad I wasn't the only one who always wears socks around the house, and that I had a special pair of Crocs just for home use.

"Who doesn't?" Jason asked, without missing a beat. "I have these UGG things you slide into. Not the boots! Don't get carried away."

Jason riffed on this one little tweet for a good couple of minutes while Dingo was in hysterics off camera. It was the kind of gold you don't get when you dive straight into a question about an artist's latest album or concert tour. I'll do just about anything to break someone from the cycle of publicist crap they repeated in their last dozen interviews. These days, people's images are curated within an inch of their lives, but I can't have that. My listeners, like me, crave authenticity and connection.

But spontaneity happens easily with someone like Blake Shelton, who's completely comfortable in his own skin and can ham it up with anyone. He once stopped me mid-sentence to say, "Hey, why do you keep staring at my hair; what's wrong with my hair?" We'll riff on that for a beat or two as Blake pretends to zhuzh up his 'do while everyone in the studio laughs. Or Keith Urban, who knows me so well we can play a bit on the air, like the time he "invited" me on tour with him and his wife, Nicole Kidman.

"OMG I'd love to come," I said. "Is this an invite from you and Nicole? Really?"

"Nope."

"Yeah," I said, pretending to be crestfallen. "That's what I thought!"

Or Dolly, who you have probably figured out by now is one of my favorite people to interview. One of the first times we spoke on camera, I accidently-on-purpose said "BoobTube" instead of YouTube, and Dolly just about fell off her chair laughing.

Juicy Sound Bites

In between, as the next song plays, we edit, chop, and come up with clever teases and wraps. A twenty-minute radio interview with Darius Rucker, for example, will get broken up into two-minute segments or highlights. Later on, we repackage and create new content from the interview for social media too. Then there is the show itself, with live breaks on the air, talking and cracking jokes over the music as it fades in and out. I usually only have a few minutes to get something out of my interview subject. If it's someone like Taylor Swift, the pressure is even greater when I am sitting face-to-face with one of the biggest stars in the world, with their publicist and record label representatives looming close, breathing down my neck. To hear that in real time, I created my "Cody Cast" podcast, to give listeners a sense of how the interview went down with no edits, totally raw. But for radio, in between the chatter, I'm rewinding and cutting the interview up, to edit out that long pause or breath, anything that detracts from the content. Under the clock I'll whip around during a commercial break and edit as much as a couple dozen times, going down to that last half of a second and driving my producers crazy with my OCD ways. It's nonstop. And that's just for radio.

Television also requires multitasking, but you must never let them see you juggling. When I am live on the red carpet for an awards show, it's like speed dating. You never know who's going to walk up to you, and you'd better have a reserve of smart, sassy questions to ask them in the thirty seconds or less before they move onto the step and repeat for their moment with the paparazzi. Any number of things can go wrong in that less controlled setting, but if I am at all distracted, I can never let it show on my face, because the viewers will know. I keep the smile on my face, and never let them see me sweat.

Professional Listener

What keeps me on point is remembering what my listeners and viewers want to hear. As a professional listener, I ask the questions I know they want the answers to. After many years of doing this job, I also instinctively know when to move onto the next subject. My audience is busy. They are bombarded with information coming at them from many different sources, so it's on me to keep them engaged and entertained so that they never turn the channel.

That's the other secret to becoming a great broadcaster: stepping outside of yourself enough to recognize that the mere sound of your voice alone won't cut it for your audience. I can empathize, because I share their low-boredom threshold. Who has time to listen to some long-winded blowhard? As a radio and television personality, you have to bring them substance wrapped up in a neat and sexy package of quick hits.

People need juicy sound bites to sink their teeth into, fun infotainment that will help them get through the monotony of their rush-hour commute or help them unwind at the end of a long, hard day. I want to bring my listeners and viewers something they can enjoy or learn from, so that they can shake off the blues and feel good.

It's about them, not me.

• LIGHTNING IN A BOTTLE •

by Dingo, Cody's longtime producer

WHEN CODY CALLED AND ASKED me to join him at CMT, I blurted out "Yes!" before he had a chance to finish his sentence.

"Wait, don't you want to know how much you'll be paid?" he asked.

I didn't care. The chance to work with Cody Alan and Brian Philips, the two best guys in the industry, was all I needed to hear. I'd left radio after The Wolf never thinking I'd go back to it. But here was my chance to have that career lightning in a bottle again. Most of us don't get to have that once in our lifetimes, much less twice.

Cody and I were given a blank canvas and all the resources we could ask for at CMT. We got to design everything from the studio to the automation. We wrote every production piece, every music bit transition, every phrase between a song. We cranked up our creative juices to describe what each show was about and say something witty or meaningful about whatever big-name star was going to turn up for an interview each night. We got to conceptualize every aspect of what we put out to our listening and viewing audiences.

For a couple of radio nerds, it was heaven, enabling the kind of creativity and quality that I am not so sure would happen today. We were coasting on the adrenaline rush of great collaboration. Cody was the visionary. I would write something for him, and he would take it a whole host of different ways and make it better. He always strove for perfection, the proof of which are the dents in my forehead from banging it on my desk at times!

I always knew Cody was going to be a big star, and I wanted to be a part of it. The Wolf could have been a Top 40 station, it was so personality driven, smart, and well written, and Cody was the leader of the pack. He had the ability to hear things before other people did, with the kind of golden ears that would have made him a genius A&R guy at a top record label.

But that skill translates perfectly into what he does today. Even though he'll prepare dozens of questions in advance of an interview, he has the ability to hear something in the artist's words and tone, know it is significant, then pivot quickly to pick up the thread and gently coax them into revealing something about themselves that fascinates our listeners. He does this in a way that's disarmingly humble. All this helps built equity in the show. Artists know they are going to get thoughtful, quality questions. They also have a comfort level with Cody from their conversations on radio that translates well to television. They don't have to be as guarded on camera because they know he's never going to abuse their trust.

Yet Cody doubts himself more than he should. When he was first asked to take over the CMT *Hot 20 Countdown*—CMT's flagship and *The Tonight Show* of countdown television—he kept hemming and hawing about the decision, wondering if he was meant for TV.

"Are you kidding me?" I told him. "This is a no-brainer!"

Cody is the equivalent of that rare five-tool baseball player—he's part of a small and elite group of broadcasters who can do it all.

(((9)))

TAKING THE LEAP

I believe you love who you love
Ain't nothin' you should ever be ashamed of.
—LUKE BRYAN, "Most People Are Good"

Walking out of the studio after our interview, my conversation with country music star Keith Urban took an unexpected turn.

"So how are *you*, mate?" he asked me with his gentle Australian lilt. "What's going on in *your* life?"

This was no casual question asked in the expectation of a quick and meaningless answer. My stock response, a chirpy, "I'm great!" wouldn't cut it this time. Up until now, as host on CMT and radio, I was the one asking all the questions. It was my job to shine the light on Nashville's hottest artists and get them to reveal some truths about themselves and their art, not share details about my own life. Besides, I always prided myself on keeping things professional, never inserting myself into the conversation, or wasting the precious time of these kings and queens of country music. But Keith seemed genuinely interested in me on a human level, and as he turned his gaze on me, I found myself revealing things I never would have dreamed of disclosing to anyone outside my inner circle of close family and friends.

"Oh, you know, I'm okay," I told him. "Working through a few things and trying to get right with myself."

Keith, who'd known me long enough to realize there was more, probed a little further.

"Oh yeah?" he said, stopping to face me and look me in the eyes. It was his subtle invitation to keep talking, so I did.

"I've been struggling; struggling because . . . I'm gay."

As the words tumbled out, I couldn't believe I was saying them. This was a secret I'd fought my whole life to keep, even from myself. But there wasn't even a nanosecond of awkward pause or regret. Keith immediately reached out and gave me a huge hug, a warm embrace that demonstrated acceptance of who I am. In all my years as a closeted gay man, I'd always imagined my truth would be met with an expression of bewilderment, derision, or disgust. Yet with one kind and heartfelt gesture, he made me feel like I was a long-lost brother who'd found his way home, and in that powerful moment of connection between one human being and another, I knew I'd be okay. Keith Urban was on my side.

There was something about the way he asked the question, remaining silent and patient, that made me *want* to open up. A lot of people would have tried to be sentence grabbers and coax it out of me based on their assumptions. Or quickly change the subject and make it about themselves. But Keith was comfortable in that space. He created an opening that allowed me to speak my truth in what felt like a safe, judgment-free zone.

Up until that point, the country music scene had been one of those last bastions of homophobia, or so I thought. I didn't see anyone like me in my industry, and I feared rejection if I didn't live up to the image I had created for myself of a red-blooded, all-American, churchgoing, God-fearing family man. I was afraid that coming out and showing the world my true self would amount to career suicide and that, somehow, I'd no longer fit, and the fans and artists would turn away from me. But I was wrong.

"It's okay, brother," Keith told me. "We're all going through something. I'm here for you if you need me."

And I knew he meant it. I've always felt a special connection to Keith, ever since I first interviewed him as a country music DJ in Dallas in the early 2000s. He's made no secret of the fact that he's had his own struggles with drugs and alcohol, which he's overcome through the love and support of his wife, Nicole. He gets what it's like to feel like the underdog, and his honesty and empathy permeate his lyrics, which often felt like they were speaking to me directly. But never more so than the text he wrote to me later that night:

"So good to see you today. This life is about people you can lean on and I want you to know that I am one that you can. It's all about the spirit and the soul. And in the words of Lin-Manuel Miranda: 'Love is love is love is love!'"

That was the moment it became so clear to me that I could do this. I could jump off this cliff and finally be free to fly. I could make this last leap toward living my most authentic life, and the people who know me and trust me would support me, whatever was to come. I didn't have to hide anymore. I could be true to myself as well as the world around me. I could be . . . happy.

Open Arms

So why was it anyone's business? Why did it matter? Because it was stopping me from building those deeper bonds, which, after all, is why we're here. I threw myself into my faith in part because I was driven to connect with others on a spiritual level. Again, from the time I could crawl, I've always been curious about people, wanting to know what made them happy, and how I could help. I was drawn to the mission-driven aspect of Mormonism because it gave me the opportunity to spread the gospel and make a difference in the lives of total strangers. But if I continued to hide a fundamental part of who I am, there would always be a barrier between me and the rest of the world. I had so many great acquaintances, but very few real friends. I shunned situations like intimate dinner parties where I might be tempted to let my guard down. I bit my tongue so many times I've got scar tissue. And boy, was it lonely.

Fast-forward to today, and I get to experience the Keith Urban hug—that warm rush of joy in the moment of total acceptance— almost daily. The people of Nashville have flung their arms open wide. After coming out, I've been blessed to receive public words of love and support from folks like Carrie Underwood, Toby Keith, Little Big Town, Darius Rucker, Dan + Shay, Kacey Musgraves, and Dierks Bentley. Now I don't stop myself from making a joke about my sexuality. There's no more self-censorship. I can cut up with my neighbors or random strangers who now know my journey without fear of who is listening in or judging. I can step out with the man I love. I can be me.

Of course, there were a few steps I needed to take before I could be all the way out there. Coming out is an evolution, not a revolution. It took a few stumbles and strides to get me to this place, living the life of a proud and openly gay man. So, it was a question of figuring out who I was, and what I wanted from a romantic partner. What kind of person did I see myself building a life with? He had big shoes to fill.

I'd already had a great partner in Terresa, so I knew what that kind of devotion and support looked and felt like. I also wanted a man, not a boy—someone grounded, and confident. The man of my dreams had to check a lot of boxes before I could feel comfortable including him in my world. He had to be more than okay with the fact that I had certain responsibilities: children, an ex-wife, and extended family who depended on me. I wanted someone who could handle all I would bring to a relationship and stand tall beside me.

Real Men

Growing up, I had plenty of male role models, starting with my father. Men who were strong, but not afraid to show their loving side. My grandfather on my mother's side was a no-nonsense, hardworking, deep-voiced, manly man. When he spoke in his booming baritone, it meant something, and you couldn't help but pay attention to every word. He had a moral command that no one questioned.

I looked up to him, figuratively and literally, because, with his long limbs and powerful arms, he seemed like a giant to me as I was growing up. Even though he cut an intimidating figure, Grandpa was humble, gentle, and kind. He was also a great listener. I could be a little chatterbox around him, but he'd smile, nod, and chuckle to himself whenever I said something ridiculous, interjecting once in a while just to correct me or impart some knowledge that was relevant in the moment. It showed me he wasn't just humoring me. He was paying attention. He always let me be myself while offering me the perspective of his experience. Having that example as a child made an impression on me and was another one of the early lessons that made me the communicator I am today.

Grandpa also set the example for loving-kindness, even though his generation was one of some prejudice. He lived to take care of his family. He was once a tobacco farmer, always busy working with his hands, fixing something on the farm or ploughing fields. Each summer, when I stayed with them in the country, I used to follow him around the property like an eager puppy, waiting for him to drop the occasional pearl of grandfatherly wisdom. He taught me how to run a lawn mower and change the oil in my car. Helping him with chores, riding the tractor, listening to my Walkman, listening to the radio, and working on the land was my summertime bliss.

Grandpa was a deeply spiritual old-school Southern Baptist. He was all about loving thy neighbor and doing what was right, even when that path was strewn with rocks and boulders. My grandparents suffered a lot when the industry fell apart. The old tobacco barn got torn down, and I'm sure money was tight. He became a long-haul trucker to make ends meet, before suffering a heart attack and retiring early. I'm not sure what disappointed him more—the loss of his livelihood or the fact that his grandson became a Mormon. I don't think he ever got over that one, and I'm not entirely sure what he'd make of the fact that his grandson is gay, but I love and miss him fiercely all the same.

My childhood hero passed in 2011. Singer Riley Green's song "I Wish Grandpas Never Died" rings true to me. There is something special about the bond between grandfather and grandson, a love spanning three generations. Since his death, I've slightly revised my definition of a real man—someone who steps up, takes care of his family, and does the right thing no matter what. Those were values my grandfather lived by. But, from my current vantage point, I also realize that real manhood doesn't have to be the conventional picture of masculinity.

It can be straight or gay. It can look like the rodeo cowboy or fireman who saves a woman from a burning building. But it can also be the effeminate boy behind the Mac counter who goes home every night to take care of his mother who is suffering from Alzheimer's, or the country DJ who goes where few in his industry have gone before.

Quiet Strength

A real man knows how to listen. He's comfortable enough in his own skin to hear and accept someone else's truth. He stands by his own convictions, but he is humble and open enough to learn from others and embrace even those who have different ideas. He doesn't feel the need to shout his opinions and drown out anyone who might have a different point of view. He may not be the person who has the most to say. It could be the strong, silent types who open their mouths only when they have something truly important to express. A great listener knows what's worth paying attention to, and who deserves the gift of your focus, your time, and your open ears.

I was gradually gaining some clarity about what I wanted in a man as I went through the transformation from Mormon husband and father to single gay guy in the city. I was like a teenager feeling that rush of possibility. But I also paid attention to the red flags. As someone with a fairly high profile in Nashville—a "sub-lebrity" as I call myself—there were always those who were more attracted to my fame and wealth. At the same time, I didn't want someone who was afraid of revealing himself. I'd met a few friends who were unwilling to let loose. It was always one step forward and ten steps back. That got old, fast.

Then again, I wasn't fully revealing myself either. Initially, I didn't want people to know the family side of me, because I was afraid of being judged for all my baggage, and for waiting so long to come out. I knew I had to meet someone who didn't just want the surface stuff.

Call me picky. I had that movie in my head again, imagining hard what I wanted my new life to look like in the belief that I could manifest it. I started paying attention to how certain couples in country music looked on the red carpet together: Garth Brooks and Trisha Yearwood; Luke Bryan and his wife, Caroline. They looked so cute together, like the perfect match. I started looking around for more examples of people out there who seemed more like me: Neil Patrick Harris and his husband, David Burtka; or Anderson Cooper and his then partner Benjamin Maisani looking fine at a black-tie gala. *I want that!* I said to myself. I wanted to walk into a room unabashedly holding hands with a gorgeous and self-possessed manly man. *How good would that moment feel?* I wondered.

Old Soul

Then, in 2015, I met Michael Trea Smith. *Ahh . . . Trea.* We met while I was working at a pop-up Carrie Underwood concert in Atlanta (Carrie was our matchmaker!). Trea was a country fan with a special fondness for Carrie. He'd been trying to get tickets to this event, but it was sold out. Then he noticed a contest on his Twitter feed and won himself two tickets in one of the front rows at The Playhouse, an intimate venue with fewer than two hundred people in the audience. It was my good fortune that he decided to bring his friend, and not his boyfriend, that night. Their relationship was in its waning days. Trea got up the nerve to approach me and strike up a conversation. We then posed for a picture, which Trea posted on his Instagram page the next day. We began messaging each other, and the conversation hasn't stopped since.

We didn't start dating right away. Trea had some stuff to take care of, including breaking up with his boyfriend in February the following year, and we started a long-distance, platonic friendship. That was a good thing, in a way, because it meant we had the time to get to know each other on a deeper level before we got intimate. There was a lot of texting and talking and flirting before we actually stepped out together in 2016.

It's not that I wasn't immediately attracted to him. Something about him, beyond his physical hotness, gave me butterflies, but I was determined to learn more about this guy and be sure I did this right. The guy was way younger than me, so I feared a divorced man with two kids in their late teens might have been too much for him to handle.

But the more I got to know him, the more I realized that his was an old soul. I'd always been drawn to people who were steady and self-aware. One of the first things I learned about Trea was that, when he was fifteen, he'd had a near death experience. He was in a terrible accident in a pickup truck driven by his childhood best friend. They had made a U-turn and were T-boned by a large utility truck at an intersection. His best friend was killed instantly, and Trea was found unconscious in a fetal position on the floor next to the passenger seat. As the medics worked on him, Trea's heart stopped and for a few minutes he was pronounced clinically dead. It happened a few times before he made it to the hospital, where he remained in a coma for two weeks.

Trea remembers a series of vivid, strange dreams as he lay unconscious in his hospital bed, hooked up to monitors. In one dream, Trea was surrounded by his entire family, but his cousin, who was more like a brother to him, wasn't there. "Where's Logan at?" he asked in his dream. "He couldn't make it," his family members told him. A few weeks after waking up from his coma, his cousin had suddenly passed, but Trea wasn't surprised when he heard the tragic news. He somehow knew things he couldn't have possibly known, and he's been deeply intuitive ever since.

The event changed Trea, and his worldview, forever. Little did he know then that it would change my life too. Hearing of his horrific experience has helped me to better understand how to live my life in the now and appreciate every moment I've been given.

Trea had no doubt that there was more to this life than our day-to-day existence and decided to live his life to the fullest, which included coming out to his family. He spent month after painful month in physiotherapy, building back his body and re-learning how to do the simplest things, including speaking and brushing his teeth. The kindness and dedication of his nurses and therapists inspired him to go into occupational therapy himself and give back to others what had been given to him.

Meant to Be

I'd already rounded a corner of understanding what I wanted from my partner. I didn't need someone who was as intensely religious as I'd been for my entire adult life. I let loose of the stranglehold of rules and accepted that true spirituality comes in all kinds of packages. What mattered most was Trea's heart, not what church he belonged to. He was unlike anyone I'd ever met before, but he showed up at just the right time, because by then I had enough clarity to hear my heart.

When I look at Trea, I see a real man. He's lived through so much despite his age, and these tests made him stronger. He connects with people on a deep level because he can empathize. It's these qualities that make him such a great listener. When anyone engages with him in conversation, you can sense his sincere interest in what they have to say. Being with him felt natural and right. He is also my soft place to land. I've learned it's one of the attributes I need most. In my sometimes-chaotic life, coming home to his sweet and warm, soft-spoken kindness steadies me. He also says some of the most funny and outrageous things I've ever heard! One good rule of a happy relationship is having a partner who makes you laugh. Trea brought just the right balance to my life.

Thinking about both my true loves, Terresa and Trea, don't ask me how I managed to get it right in both a straight relationship and a gay relationship. Maybe that they both found me when they did is proof that God's timing is perfect.

Getting Serious

But I didn't share Trea with anyone at first. My challenge was how to tell Terresa. I wasn't worried about how Trea would handle meeting my family. He was looking forward to it and embraced everything about me I thought would be negatives in a relationship.

First, I knew it was time to come out to my kids. I decided to take each one out on their own, beginning with my stepdaughter, Lauren, who was twenty-five at the time. I made a lunch date and, when I told her, she took it in stride, getting up from the table to hug me.

"I love you no matter what," she said.

Next, my seventeen-year-old daughter, Makayla, and I went on a road trip to Alabama for a concert. The timing was intentional. My daughter would be trapped in the car with me for three hours, with no way out of talking through how she really felt about it. I shared what had been going on with me in the car, somewhere southbound on I-65. She went quiet at first, processing the news. Then she squeezed my hand and said: "I love you Dad. This doesn't change anything."

Finally, it was Landon's turn. I wasn't sure how he'd react. He was thirteen going on fourteen, which seemed like a sensitive age to tell a boy his father is into men. We grabbed some dinner and headed back to my apartment where I sat him down and told him. He hugged me and said, "You love who you love, so what? This doesn't change who you are. You're still my dad."

All three kids accepted my truth without question. I guess Terresa and I had raised some well-adjusted children, although I am not so sure we can take full credit. We always insisted on talking through their decisions with them, even when we disagreed. We always gave them the freedom to open their mouths and express their opinions without having to self-edit. If they broke the rules, we didn't send them to their rooms, at least not often. I usually sat down with them to discuss how better choices could have been made, probably to the point where they would have preferred to have been grounded. Was it that transparency and willingness to listen without judgment that they were giving to me? Were they mature beyond their years?

Or was it simply that this generation is more familiar and comfortable with the idea that human sexuality comes in all shades?

In my head, I'd played out how the conversations would go, hoping for the best but preparing myself for the worst. I'd felt nervous anticipation for weeks. But all that guilt and shame I'd carried about hiding it from them was canceled out the instant I shared my truth with them. I felt especially guilty over leaving them in Salt Lake City for days at a time. But my absences were not felt in the way I had feared. In fact, they have only happy memories of playing in the snow. Wait, what?! Didn't they even miss me a little?

Family Bowling Night

Just before I told Landon, I decided to include Trea in a family night out. This way, my son would have already experienced Trea's kindness before having to process my big news. The other purpose was to introduce Trea to Terresa. We decided to go bowling, the perfect icebreaker. Makayla and her boyfriend joined us for safety in numbers, although Terresa jokingly referred to herself as the "fifth wheel."

She had already written to Trea, who at this point was nameless and faceless to her. My ex had taken the time and trouble to compose a long, detailed email to my potential new life partner, full of sweet stories she felt Trea ought to know about who I was as a husband and father. It was a touching testimony of Terresa's love for me as her person and soul mate, and it moved me to tears. When I shared it with Trea, he cried too. The final point of her message was this:

I am giving his heart to you, and I want you to take good care of it.

When it was finally time for us all to meet up in person, Terresa confided in me that she was so nervous she felt like she was going to throw up. When we all pulled up into the parking lot of the bowling alley at the same time, Trea walked straight up to Terresa, grabbed her by both hands, looked her in the eyes, and said: "I want you to know that I am going to take good care of him, and you don't have to worry."

Then he gave her a big hug and held her hand as we walked inside. That he would tackle a sensitive subject like that the moment he met her earned Terresa's respect and gratitude. That was the real icebreaker. She was almost giddy as she got to know him and experience the warmth of his personality, not to mention his "drop-dead gorgeous" looks (her words, not mine). They talked all night, mostly dishing about me, like instant best friends.

Makayla had the same chemistry with Trea. A little closer in age, they were playful with each other, sitting off in a corner dishing about her new boyfriend, Will, and taking sneaky snapchat photos of Landon with funny filters. At one point, Trea forgot that Landon still had not been told about me, and unconsciously put his hand on my back. Landon noticed this little gesture and whispered to his mother, "I think Trea might be gay." As they were driving home, Will, who had also not yet been told, commented to Makayla, "If I didn't know better, I'd say that your dad and Trea were a couple!"

Those clues helped me to bridge the conversation I had with Landon shortly afterward. I suspect he already suspected, and had prepared himself for the news, because he reacted with an openness and maturity that was beyond his years.

Domestic Bliss

From that point on, it was easy. Not that it's always been perfect. Like any relationship, we have our moments, and my OCD ways sometimes clash when Trea casually drops a pair of his dirty socks on the floor. But my outgoing and free-spirited other half has taught me so much about self-acceptance, acceptance of others, and embracing life to the fullest. Before he came along, my life was all about striving to hit the next goal, and the next. I was always calculating and recalculating, thinking about the future and never in the moment. He's shown me how to take a big bite out of life.

It's because I've been blessed with the right guy, and a doll of an ex, that we've been able to enjoy the ultimate modern family. Everyone loves Trea almost as much as I do, to the point where he sometimes knows more about what's going on in their lives than I do. Trea and Makayla even hit the bars together, like BFFs. Trea and Terresa also chat on their own. They are similar in many ways. They are both incredibly nurturing, thinking of others before thinking about themselves, almost to a fault. Growing up, Terresa always dreamed of becoming a nurse or a caregiver like Trea. At least on some level, I can take credit for having consistent good taste!

There is nothing conventional about our life together. We all hang out at each other's homes, we spend holidays together, and even go on annual vacations: me, Trea, Terresa and her boyfriend, the kids and their boyfriend and girlfriend. For a while I was getting worried that Terresa had decided to put herself permanently on the shelf. To help her out, I wrote her profile for all the dating apps. I even helped her pick out a guy, and sure enough, she found herself a good-looking younger man who treats her like a queen.

Of course, there were yet more steps to take before I could live my life completely out loud. Parents and extended family were next. They had to be told before they read about it in the tabloids. When Terresa told her parents, aunts, uncles, and close friends, it was as if she'd solved the puzzle for them. "Well, we still love him, but that explains a lot!" her mother exclaimed. It wasn't because they have excellent "gaydar" so much as the fact that we were always together, even after our divorce. We never stopped loving each other, just in a different kind of way.

Next, I wrote an email to my mother, knowing she would share it with Dad and the rest of our family in South Carolina:

Mom,

I know what I'm about to tell you will be met with love. You have always loved me, no matter what. I learned unconditional love from YOU. You always showed this kind of love to me, Dad, Missy, Terresa and all the grandkids. I recall that, I'm now your age when you sent me to Seattle for 2 years on a Mormon mission. I can't imagine doing that now with Makayla or Landon. I don't know how you did that with such strength. You love me dearly, and I know it. Thank you for that gift.

But this may be the hardest thing I have ever had to share. It's something I've wrestled with my entire life, always thinking something was wrong with me. But I have come to realize that nothing is wrong with me because God made me. He has a purpose for me. He has a plan for everyone, obviously. And, although my path is different, and not easy, I have decided to be honest.

As you might have suspected, I am gay.

The email went on for a few more paragraphs. Even though I talk for a living, this was one occasion when I didn't trust the words to come so easily, so I was determined to write down every thought and feeling I wanted to convey to one of the most important people in my life. To my amazement, she told me she never suspected. All those childhood years of hoarding men's underwear catalogs underneath my bed somehow escaped her attention. My anxiousness to grab the mail each month to make sure I tucked away the latest copy to avoid prying eyes or questions didn't even raise an eyebrow. I must have been a better actor than I thought. But my big revelation was met with nothing but total acceptance. Mom, Dad, and the rest of my family told me how proud they were, and that they loved me no matter what. It was all I needed to hear.

The next step was telling the world. The love and support of Trea, Terresa, my kids, my parents, and a tight inner circle of friends gave me the strength to finally take the leap, go public, and use my outside voice. Not that my coming out was a foregone conclusion. It's like Ellen explained when she talked about coming out on the final episode of her sitcom: "The people around you already know, so you don't just say the words 'I'm gay' in a normal conversation. And once you say it in front of millions of people, that's it. There's no going back." She danced around it. There were a lot of teasers. I can't say my situation was exactly the same, because that was twenty years ago, and unlike Ellen, I wasn't getting death threats. But it was scary enough—like facing down your first bungee jump when you're really not sure if the cord will hold.

When I was considering how to break such news, my friend Olympian Gus Kenworthy reminded me of words that are often attributed to Dr. Seuss, which in a poignant yet whimsical way completely describe the best approach:

Be who you are and say what you feel, because those who mind don't matter and those who matter don't mind.

Luckily for me, there were enough people in my life, like Keith Urban, as well as a tight circle of gay friends—my tribe—who listened and made me feel understood. This little crew of mine created the necessary space and patiently waited in silence for me to speak my truth. Those pauses in the conversation can be an important part of the communication, which can come to an abrupt halt when someone feels the need to fill the void with a silly joke or observation. Just like a great song has a rhythm and spaces between the lyrics, so does a meaningful exchange between two people. It can be incredibly hard to say certain things, but you make it easier for the other person when you are patient and open. Silence creates an opening, a sacred zone in the middle where the two of you can meet. The people who loved me gave me that gift. They built that bridge by letting my truth come to them on my terms, and at my own pace. Now I could hear myself and others loud and clear, unmuffled by all those years of denial.

Final Freak-Out

Of course, I was a hot mess in the days leading up to my decision to go public. On a work trip to New York with my producer and friend Dingo, he sat in my hotel room with me and listened as I went back and forth on the subject for hours.

"You are who you are, and you shouldn't hide from that. Just be the best version of yourself," he told me.

The night before I planned to leap, I was pacing the living room of our Nashville home like a maniac. Trea sat me down on our couch and said: "I am not with you for whatever you can give me, but because I love you, so you don't need to do this for me. Just ask yourself what *you* want. Either way, I'll support you."

Hearing his words gave me the final hit of clarity I needed. I was doing this for me, so that I could live my life out and proud, but it was also for a reason bigger than myself.

"I guess if I am able to say that I am gay and country, it will help who knows how many gay kids in small towns across America."

"Then," Trea said, "accept that answer inside of you and be at peace with it. I'll be right here with you, no matter what. Just know there's no way to un-jump, if you wanna fly!"

Each reaction of love spurred me on, including the acceptance of artists and friends. So many seminal moments finally gave me the courage to tell the world in a *People* article and in a January 2017 Instagram post:

As we start a new year, there is something I want to share with you. You see, I'm gay. This is not a choice I made, but something I've known about myself my whole life. Through life's twists and turns, marriage, divorce, fatherhood, successes, failures—I've landed on this day, a day when I'm happier and healthier than I've ever been. And I'm finally comfortable enough for everyone to know this truth about me. Thanks for following me and supporting me over the years. As we continue our journey, I hope this news won't change how you see me. I'm still the same Cody I always was. You just know a little more about me now. My hope for the future is to live the most honest, authentic, loving, and open life possible. Here's to being happy with yourself, no matter who you are, who you love, where you come from, or what cards life has dealt you. Thanks again. With much heart, Cody

There it was: my decades-long secret released into the universe. The reactions were overwhelmingly positive. For every one thousand or so comments on social media, there may have been one sour note. The outpouring of love and support came from some places I didn't expect. Toby Keith, someone I thought of as a good ol' boy alpha country male, and whose potential reaction made me nervous, shared my post with this comment: *I admire your courage.* Carrie, of course, had this to tweet: *So much love and respect for you, sweet Cody! You are one of the kindest human beings I know. I wish you nothing but happiness!* Dierks Bentley honored me with these words: *proud of you dude. happiness is found in the most authentic form of ourselves. carry on!* Darius Rucker added: *I love you man. So happy you know who you are. Proud to call you my friend. Much love!!!*

A month later, in February 2017, I went to visit my father for the last time. My mother had already shared my news with him, and his reaction was nothing but love and acceptance. When I brought Trea to meet him, Dad was weak, but he sat up in his bed, cheerful as ever and excited to get to know my fella.

"You're a part of this family now," he told him, then gave him the biggest bear hug he could muster.

To me, he simply said: "I'm proud of you, Son."

Today, I enjoy a relationship with my community and my industry that's more authentic. Being able to communicate without a filter allows me to be more spontaneous and present to others. I've learned that going public with my inner turmoil has inspired others. One of the things that had been holding me back was my fear that this news could ruin my hard-won career in country music, but I could not have been more wrong, because our shows' ratings have never been better.

Sharing this side of myself has deepened my connection with viewers and listeners, and they're tuning in more than ever. I've heard from adults and kids all over the country who no longer feel so alone. Sharing my experiences of listening and being truly heard also lets them know they *can* put the truth about their authentic selves out into the world. Among the many messages I've received since coming out was this one from an Army soldier named Dusty:

I just wanted to say thank you. I'm thirty-one, as country as it gets and gay. Not out yet though. Anyway, I just figured I'd have to live this lie the rest of my life. Stuck somewhere between pretending to be normal and hating myself. Then I read your story of coming out later in life and I realized that maybe there is another path. Maybe I can be happy someday too.

Eric wrote:

It's so nice to see that both country music and a gay man can coexist. You have reenergized my love for country but more importantly, you have set a great example of being happy and free in your own skin. Thanks for standing up despite standing out. As a fellow gay man and a country music fan, I owe ya one!

Jackie's message said:

I started following you when you came out. As a lesbian, I look up to you because I know how bold a decision it is to come out, especially in your position. Thanks and welcome to the family!

Another message, from Brandon, reads:

For years I have watched you on CMT and then started following you on Instagram and have enjoyed your presence in the country music world. I just want to let you know how much your coming out influenced me and showed me that no matter what and/or where you are in life, love will win!

Again, you just never know who is listening, or how your actions will impact individuals from all walks of life. A case in point: Colton Underwood, a star of the hit reality show *The Bachelor* and a former NFL player. I'd met Colton in Las Vegas at the 2019 ACM Awards, and we hit it off right away. He knew me from CMT, and admittedly, I'm a fan of *The Bachelor*, having crushed on him while watching the latest season of the show. Later we met up, along with his then girlfriend, in Mexico for Luke Bryan's country music festival. I had no clue he was gay.

But in April 2021, he came out to a flurry of headlines. Right before he took his leap, he called me. We talked about being at the festival in Mexico, and how he had few gay friends and felt like I was one of the only gay guys he could relate to. He told me that I helped inspire his bold decision. So much so that he wanted me to be part of the filming of those final moments before he came out, for his new series documenting his experience.

Colton flew to Nashville, along with our mutual acquaintance Gus Kenworthy. I invited Colton and Gus over to our house for dinner, and it was a night of great food and conversation, made all the better with margaritas, wine, and music from gay country singer Cody Belew. We talked about all the facets of being gay and, more specifically, what's it's like to come out. That was when Colton revealed that observing Trea and me in Mexico, as well as our strolls on the red carpet, looking so relaxed and happy together, enabled him to visualize that happiness for himself. What a perfect full-circle moment!

A few days later, Colton sat down for an interview with *Good Morning America*'s Robin Roberts. Robin seemed like the right person to do the interview with Colton. After all, Robin and I once talked being gay in the media, and she told me, "We've all got something we're going through. Make your mess your message!"

For the first time, Colton spoke publicly, and his words hit me hard:

"I ran from myself for a long time. I've hated myself for a long time. I'm gay," he told Robin and the world.

Most of us who are gay have felt this way for much of our lives—even running from the very word *gay*. Yet nowadays saying "I'm gay" has become a badge of honor and something I'm proud of.

That I can be an inspiration to someone like Colton brings me joy. It's also thrilling and inspiring to see others walk this path. Early in 2021, Brothers Osborne lead singer T.J. Osborne made his leap. A tall drink of water with classic cowboy good looks, T.J. is built in the mold of a classic country music star. The real-life brothers duo has a string of awards for real Wolf-style rockin' country anthems. Likely, T.J.'s coming out as gay was the last thing his fans expected. He's been candid about his concerns over how he'll be received in a mainstream music market that leans conservative. After all, T.J. is the first country music artist signed to a major record label at the peak of his career to make this move, and I have full admiration for the guy. I get what he must've been going through, but I also believe he will be embraced in ways he never imagined. If there is one thing I would tell him, it's this:

Yes, you can be a country-music-loving, red-meat-eating, cowboy-boot-wearing, God-loving, foot-stomping gay man. There's a lot of identity politics going on right now, and people get ruffled when you express ideas that don't quite fit with whatever "team" you're supposed to be on. But that's okay. You don't have to look and sound like everyone else. Human beings are complex creatures and I believe there's room for all of us on this planet if only we'd take the time to listen to one another. The more expansive we allow ourselves to be, the more open we are to hearing out different or surprising points of view, the more tolerant and less polarized our world can become. And the less alone you feel. That's why I wouldn't un-jump, even if I could.

• DREAMS COME TRUE •

by Trea, Cody's partner

I WAS SO NERVOUS THE night I met Terresa and the kids. Nervous, but excited. I had three whiskey Cokes just to calm myself down, and it must have worked because the moment we got together in person it just felt right. Terresa had written to me beforehand, welcoming me into the family, and I was deeply touched by it. One of the things she told me in her note was that "Cody will change your life and make all your dreams come true!" I loved Terresa and her big blonde hair from the moment I saw her.

Things were getting serious between me and my new man. We'd already had a romantic getaway and we were talking about me moving to Nashville, even though I'd sworn to myself I'd never move for a man. But Cody was different. Even though we were years apart in age, it was as if our paths were meant to converge. I'd already been through a lot, from my nearly fatal accident, personal losses, and a series of unhealthy relationships. I went through a period of depression, or PTSD, drinking hard and being promiscuous just to feel something. But by the time I met Cody, I was clear in my head about what

I did and did not want. I'd been through hell and back and was ready for a good man to be my only one.

I found my person, someone I could be in a healthy, adult relationship with. We have more fun together sitting on the couch and watching a good movie than hanging out in a gay bar. Then again, we're not just homebodies. By the time I came along, Cody was ready to let loose and enjoy a drink or two.

I guess you could say I was Cody's "gay guide" in the gay world. I took him to his first gay strip club, and his jaw fell to the floor.

"It's legal to do that?!" he asked me.

"Just relax and enjoy it," I told him.

We saved each other. And we balance each other. When he gets wound up and starts beating up on himself, I talk him down. And when I get low, worrying or grieving over one of my elderly patients, he lifts me up. We are the yin to each other's yang.

When Cody made that leap and came out to the world, I was so proud to walk with him on the red carpet. It was our first public appearance together after the big announcement and I felt like I was in a movie surrounded by all those beautiful people, light bulbs flashing in our faces. I held his hand and felt him tremble a little, but as we stopped at the step and repeat, posing for the press, no one said, "Oh, it's that gay couple," as I expected. We weren't treated like the token gay couple. Instead, they called us by our names, Cody and Trea, just like everybody else!

((**10**))

SIX FEET APART

There will come a day
When the tears and the sadness, the pain and the hate
The struggle, this madness, will all fade away.
—CARRIE UNDERWOOD, "Love Wins"

We slept through the storm. Well, that's probably an understatement, because the deadly tornado that ripped through parts of Nashville on the night of March 2, 2020, was a monster that mowed through entire neighborhoods, flattening buildings and turning them into mulch. One of those buildings happened to be the apartment that Trea and I had moved out of just four months earlier. Our former home was on the top floor, with huge floor-to-ceiling windows. Had we still been there, we could have lost everything, including our lives. A few friends and associates didn't know that we'd already moved into our new house just a mile away from the tornado's path in Sylvan Heights and they were alarmed. At 1:30 a.m., we were woken up by the nonstop pinging of our phones.

We quickly scrolled down our text messages to make sure our loved ones were okay. My ex, Terresa, and our kids live in Franklin, far enough from the devastation, but we checked in with each other just in case. It was obvious as I checked the Twitter and Instagram feeds that the same weather system had struck at least twice through east and northeast Nashville and Mount Juliet, the exact same trajectory as Nashville's last big "Super Outbreak" of twisters in 1974. How freaky was that?

Trea and I switched on the local news for more updates. The enormity of what had just happened struck us when we learned that twenty-five people had been killed, including five children. Our former home and stomping ground of Germantown, a cute neighborhood with restored Victorian architecture, a farmers market, and chic sidewalk cafés, had suffered some of the worst damage, including two streets that were completely wiped out. Of course, there was no way we could get back to sleep for the rest of the night, so we both just stared at our phones, examining each photo of the wreckage. As soon as the sun rose, we went up on our deck to survey the damage for ourselves. Mother Nature had wreaked so much havoc less than a mile from our new home.

Viral Telethon

The Nashville community has a history of coming together after a calamity. When the whole town, including the Grand Ole Opry, was underwater from flooding in 2010, just months after I moved here, country music celebrities got together and raised millions to repair the damage. We mobilized swiftly this time too. Two days later, on March 5, CMT and Nashville's local NBC affiliate, WSMV-TV, cosponsored a telethon to raise funds for the American Red Cross's Southern Tornado and Flood Relief Program, aired live from CMT's downtown Nashville studio where I worked. I was one of the cohosts, and for three hours that evening celebrity after celebrity dropped by to man the phones, share personal stories, and encourage viewers to pledge to help out Middle Tennessee: Lady A's Charles Kelley and Dave Haywood, Travis Denning, Devin Dawson, Blanco Brown, Cassadee Pope, Gavin DeGraw, Kalie Shorr, Sam Palladio, Sarah Darling, Whitney Duncan, and many more. We raised close to $400,000 by the end of the night.

There wasn't a murmur among us about coronavirus. We'd been so preoccupied with our local disaster that a global disaster didn't even enter into our thoughts. Until the next day when I got a call from someone at Viacom/CBS's human resources department (Viacom/CBS owns CMT):

"Cody, you have to quarantine for two weeks," she told me.

"What?! Why?!" I asked, thinking it must be some kind of joke.

"Someone tested positive for coronavirus at the tornado telethon, so anyone who attended has to stay home and self-quarantine. Please report back to us if you have any symptoms."

Immediately my phone started blowing up again. All those who participated had been asked to think about who we came into close contact with, so we were urgently comparing notes. When I reviewed the footage of the telethon, I realized there wasn't anyone I *didn't* come into close contact with. That's just the nature of our affectionate, never-afraid-to-hug country music crowd. Everyone was embracing each other and kissing. I saw myself leaning over to whisper in someone's ear, probably

one of the most effective methods of spreading a highly contagious virus. Although I felt no symptoms, I spent the next few
days worried I was Typhoid Mary, contaminating some of the
leading lights of my industry. Luckily, there were no further
reports of infection.

At first, I was mostly just annoyed by the inconvenience. I
was also pissed off that I wouldn't be able to go to work. That
same week, I was to receive a Visibility Award from the Human
Rights Campaign, an organization that's been at the forefront
of LGBTQ+ rights, and the gala in Nashville was a big deal to
me. The work I'd been doing to raise awareness for this and
other organizations counted among my greatest passions, and
none other than my longtime friend Kelsea Ballerini was to
present the award to me. But Cinderella Cody would not be
allowed to go to the ball this time, even though she had the
perfect outfit already picked out. Part of being gay is that you
plan well ahead for these nights.

I have stuff to do, man! I thought. *I was robbed!*

But the more information trickled in, the more I understood
how serious this was. I wasn't going to be missing anything,
because two days later, the gala was canceled, and the entire
world was on lockdown. Life as we knew it had come to a hard
stop. Two *weeks* later, we also learned that this invisible danger
wasn't going away in a couple of weeks. I had to figure this out
for the foreseeable future because, in the middle of all this
chaos and uncertainty, I figured my listeners needed the comfort of a familiar voice. And I needed the comfort of being able
to listen to them and be heard beyond the confines of my home.
As unsettling as all this was, I needed my country music community to get through whatever this was with some sense of
normalcy.

Within twenty-four hours of the lockdown notice, my CMT team swung into action. They brought over all the equipment, set up the radio equipment and microphones on my kitchen table and the lighting and cameras in my dining room. I got a crash course on how to be a one-man show on radio and TV and prayed that when the time to go live came I would know which buttons to push.

All that busy-ness kept me from thinking too hard about how scary the pandemic was. We didn't have time to panic-buy toilet paper or Purell. At no point in the early phase of the lockdown did it occur to me to be particularly worried about my own health. Of course, I was concerned about my mom, who was at a high-risk age, but I knew she was staying at home in South Carolina, and that my nephews, both young men, were with her, going to the store and taking good care of her. Terresa and my own kids were also safe and well.

Trea was the loved one who had me most worried. Not necessarily because he might get sick, because he was a fit and healthy guy, but because his job as an occupational therapist at an assisted-living home meant he could put his elderly patients at risk. Every day he went into work, changed into an entirely different set of clothes, and layered up with a hazmat suit and personal protective equipment (PPE). The man was working directly with COVID patients, in the COVID unit, and you could not get more front line than that. Aware that this was a highly contagious disease, Trea was scrupulous about safety, showering and washing his clothes at work, even switching his shoes, then coming home from each shift and doing the same. The thought of spreading the virus was devastating. Trea would much rather have the illness himself than pass it along to others, and that fear hung over us both.

Home Studio

After a few weeks of this new routine, it was apparent that my way of working would not be going back to normal anytime soon, so I had to come up with a more sustainable way of doing my shows from home without dragging my germs all the way across town. Besides, I was getting sick of staring at all the wires, boards, and laptops in my new kitchen.

The other hazard of working that way was the close proximity of Little Debbie cakes and potato chips (at least I found the time to stock up on lockdown snacks, along with seventeen cans of Chunky soup, which I'm pretty sure are still in my pantry, untouched). A month into it, I noticed I was packing on more than a few pounds. It was hard not to when I had to look at myself on Zoom video all day. My solution was to convert one-half of our two-car garage into a home gym and get busy with the weights. I also decided to turn the guest bedroom, several steps and one flight of stairs away from the fridge, into my home office. My sanity and my thirty-one-inch waistline depended on it.

It was hard to believe that just a couple of months before, none of us had ever even heard of Zoom, and now it's a verb, like Uber or Google. It completely transformed the way I work. In my little spare bedroom, I was able to set up a radio and TV studio using my laptop, my iPhone, a couple of tripods, and the trusty ring light, one of many delivery purchases from Walmart. com. I took Trea's dining table from his old apartment and set it up as a desk, invested in a swivel chair, and created a backdrop with shelving to display a bunch of cool stuff like my ACM awards, a "Favorite Dad" baseball from my son, Landon, some books, my portrait of Dolly Parton inscribed with WWDD (What Would Dolly Do?), and a rock I'd pilfered from a park in Alaska a couple of years earlier, just enough treasures for the background shot, to say a little something about me without being too distracting.

I was back to being the boy in his bedroom playing with Mr. Microphone, albeit with much more expensive technology. Although I missed seeing my team in person every day, part of me dug the fact that I could get out of bed and be just thirty-seven steps from work. Beyond that, I relished the challenge, adapting the format of the show, going from analog to digital, in-person to virtual, in a matter of days.

The setup was perfect. I had three broadcasting stations within inches of each other. I just had to swivel to my right, where I had a monitor and a big camera in the corner. When I swiveled a notch to my left, I faced the radio mic, then my Zoom camera, which was actually my iPhone set up on a tripod under the ring light, a circular light that compensated for the fact that I had no makeup people on hand to airbrush the flaws away. For any of you thinking about getting filler or Botox after too many depressing reflections of yourself on a Zoom conference call, try a ring light first. It's much cheaper!

Teddy Time

The other important prop inside the home studio was my dog, Teddy, a golden retriever pup who snoozed at my feet all day when I wasn't giving him his long morning walks in the nearby hills. Over the months, Teddy became a kind of mascot for the show. In fact, he was more like a social media superstar with his own Instagram account: @NasvilleTeddy. We even created a segment on the show called "Teddy Time" where my dog had playdates with the pets of the celebrities I was interviewing. I got the stars to introduce their animals and Zoom in with me and Teddy, showing us tricks and eating their favorite treats. One guest was Mitchell Tenpenny's rescue dog, Annie, who got her name from the Zac Brown Band song "Sweet Annie." Annie was sweet, and Mitchell shared how much comfort she brought him during the lockdown.

California country singer Jon Pardi showed off his fur babies live from his farm just outside of Nashville. From the looks of it, they're spoiled by Jon and his wife, Summer, as Gus, Charlie, Bear, and Cowboy enjoyed a massive spread of land during the lockdown and beyond. This Teddy Time appropriately began with Jon exclaiming, "Release the beasts!"

Another Teddy Time guest was Runaway June, or, rather, Naomi Cooke, Natalie Stovall, and Jennifer Wayne.

"This is the show where we not only introduce the stars and their dogs, but also do some heavy petting! Heavy petting is encouraged," I explained to the girls as they presented their fur babies and Teddy licked my post-first walk, sweaty leg.

Since Naomi has no pets, we were joined by Natalie's animal brood, which consisted of her fourteen-year-old pooch, Cinnamon, some sort of Chihuahua mix with a few gray whiskers around her muzzle, and her Heinz 57 rescue, Brady Bell. Jennifer's rescue dogs were the adorable mutt Beau, who was swept off the mean streets of East Nashville to lock down in luxury in Malibu with his siblings; Spike, a funny-looking, small yellow dog; and Little Blue, an overfed, seventeen-pound Chihuahua. Little Blue showed us a trick, standing up on her hind legs for a treat. It was clear how she got to be seventeen pounds!

Teddy Time, bringing the dogs of the country music world together, is just one of many ways I was trying to bring my listeners more comfort food for their ears and eyes through social media. Of course, I want to make clear that cats were always welcome. I'm still hoping to get Taylor Swift and her cat Olivia Benson on Teddy Time. We don't discriminate!

Did I miss doing my interviews in person? Hell to the yes! I feed off the energy of the people in the room with me. And there were all those little moments with the artist off the air, walking them to and from the studio, where they would reveal something about themselves, that I was no longer privy to. I also am always quick to observe their wardrobe, new tattoos, or even fragrances that might be fun to talk about on air. But our new, hermetically sealed existence meant I'd have to work much harder to find that level of intimacy.

I also missed the awards shows. Each year, the country music industry recognizes its artists through three platforms: the Academy of Country Music (ACM), which normally takes place in April; the CMT Awards (country music's best night out), which typically happens in June; and the Country Music Association (CMA) Awards Show, which in past years happened in November. In 2020, all these shows would be clustered together over a few weeks in the fall.

In March 2020, when I was discussing the impact of coronavirus on the industry during an interview with Dierks Bentley, we were talking about the fact that all these shows would be jam-packed together, and he asked me, "Do you really think they're going to happen?"

"Sure," I told him. "That's months away!"

I joked that I would wear the same suit to all three shows, to save myself the time and trouble of picking out three.

"Man, if all those shows happen, I will buy you a new suit to wear to all the shows!" Dierks promised me, half-seriously. "When people ask you who you're wearing on the red carpet, you can tell them it's 'Dierks Bentley.'"

Comfort Food

Until those fall awards shows, by when I figured this COVID thing had to be over, there would be a lot of changes to my old format. We worked with what we had and, in a way, the "new normal" was just what I needed to shake me out of my rut. When you get proficient at something, it's almost as if you are relying on muscle memory. You take certain things for granted. You're not always present in the moment. So, by necessity, I had to press the *reset* button, which wasn't a bad thing.

It was a question of balance. I wanted to acknowledge what was going on in our world. At the same time, I wanted to bring the comfort food of dad jokes, pop culture, and a smattering of silliness so that my listeners could get a break from the endless stream of bad news and doom scrolling on the internet. People needed somewhere to turn for a reassuring tone and a sense that somehow, some way, this, too, would pass.

In radio, we create fun jingles and one-liners to blast in between segments. We adapted our format, punctuating our shows with a line from Luke Combs's song about the pandemic: "Someday when we aren't six feet apart." It's a hopeful, poignant song on its own, but put that line in the context of my broadcast, and there was some intended humor to it. We also used the phrase "Siiil-Ver Liii-Nings!" to highlight the scraps of positive news or inspiration we could share with our listeners. We knew it was a cliché, so we played it up, announcing it like the latest score at a ballpark, to wink at our audience and laugh at ourselves.

Every hour I also paid tribute to the frontline workers, a subject obviously dear to my heart, with a recording of the noisemakers, whistles, and cheers that went out whenever health care workers changed shifts at the hospital. This "Here's to the

Heroes" segment paid tribute to listeners who were nurses, doctors, EMTs, truck drivers, military personnel, grocery store workers, delivery truck drivers, you name it. We invited these fans to call in and share what they were going through. I was on a mission to celebrate these folks and share as many positive, inspiring stories as I could.

Rich Soil

The music itself also gave comfort. Just as the soil in a field gets richer when it's been left to lie fallow for a time, 2020 was an intensely creative moment for many of our artists. Because they weren't constantly on the move with their concert tours, they were forced to turn inward, writing songs inside their home studios during the lockdown, with lyrics that expressed a little or a lot of what we were all going through, from Big & Rich's "Stay Home," a silly song about searching for toilet paper and homeschooling to make us laugh through the fear, to Thomas Rhett's "Be a Light," an uplifting, spiritual tune featuring a pantheon of country stars like Reba McEntire, Keith Urban, and Hillary Scott.

Dolly's wistful "When Life Is Good Again" gave me resolve and hope. Adam Hambrick wrote "Between Me and the End of the World" to honor his wife, who was on the front lines treating COVID-19 patients as a physical assistant. *"It's a hell of a thing watching you stand in between / Between me and the end of the world,"* was one of many lines that struck a chord with me, and Trea.

The country artists were experiencing the full array of human emotions about this epidemic, and country songs were the perfect way to channel these natural responses to what we were going through. Some of the music voiced the anger and frustration so many were feeling weeks into the lockdown, with millions out of work, and small business owners struggling to keep the lights on, like Chris Janson's workingman anthem "Put Me Back to Work":

Trucks still gotta drive / People still gotta thrive / Open up the doors and fill the seats / 'Cause people still gotta eat.

Although some thought the lyrics were a political statement, Chris shared with *Billboard* magazine his inspiration for the song:

A few weeks ago, I met a neighbor who had just lost his son to suicide from being out of work. Not only was it heartbreaking, but I'd heard other stories just like his. I was thinking about the hurt and the struggles that so many of us are feeling right now. So, I woke up the next morning heavy-hearted and did what I do: I wrote.

Seeing the authentic way country music reflected so many aspects of how we were all feeling reminded me of other touch points in history, like after 9/11 when Alan Jackson sang, "Where were you when the world stopped turning on that September day?" Our music has always had a way of matching the emotions of the moment.

Silver Linings

It was my mission to present these sincere expressions of human emotion that connected us all, as well as songs that were already written yet somehow seemed appropriate for the times. I didn't believe it was my role to address the issues head-on. The music could do that. Folks tuned into my broadcasts for a lightening of their load. If they were carrying a lot of rocks, I wanted to take away a few of them to make their climb just a little bit easier.

Of course, I acknowledged what was going on and how people were feeling. You can be positive without being glib. And there was plenty to be grateful for. Almost every artist I spoke with shared how they would never get this kind of time with family again with all the running coast to coast and concert to concert, being on tour bus every single weekend. There was a sweetness to being home all the time, which I felt myself. Not only was it a pleasant change not to be on a plane or in some hotel room all the time, I got to focus on my kids more than I ever could when they were growing up. Being able to tune into them as they were becoming young adults was another blessing.

Makayla was something of a social butterfly as she pursued her career in Nashville. The lockdown required her to press *pause* on her lifestyle, at least for a while, and content herself with fluttering her wings on social media instead. We benefited from being in proximity to her joyful energy. Selfishly, I enjoyed the fact that Trea and I got more movie nights, cookouts, and sit-down family dinners.

That precious time also allowed me to focus more of my energy on my son, Landon, who was attending a prestigious music academy as COVID hit. Landon's like me in a lot of ways, an extroverted introvert. He's more than capable of being social, but his happy place is alone in his room, making music for emerging artists (hip-hop, pop, country, any genre) while generally being a music nerd. Like father, like son. As the lockdown continued, I started noticing he seemed lethargic and a little down. Every day was Blursday, and Landon was spending a little too much time alone. When I knocked on his door during a visit to Terresa's house, I could see why. His space looked like a dungeon, cluttered and dark, not helped by the fact that he never opened his curtains. We talked about how he was feeling and why.

Because I was no longer always on the go, I noticed things I might have missed pre-COVID, and could slow down long enough to really hear my son. He, like a lot of young people living through this crisis, was scared for his future and wondering if he'd ever be able to have a successful career and branch out on his own. He had already been experiencing some success for years, making money from his growing production business, but the constant doom and gloom on the news made him question what was out there for him in the long term. He felt stuck, with nothing to look forward to, something no young person should ever have to feel. But I had a hunch I knew how to improve his outlook.

"Landon, I know it seems like so much is beyond your control, but there is one thing that is within your power," I told him.

"What's that?"

"Your environment! We should fix up your room a little bit and bring a little sunshine in here!" Suddenly, I became Cam, the flamboyant gay father from the show *Modern Family*.

I guess this is the one stereotypically gay trait of mine, besides an abiding love for drag queens. I do love to decorate and have done so ever since I was a little boy, rearranging my parents' living room to perfect its feng shui. If a poster on my wall was a little crooked or frayed, it drove me crazy, and Mom never had to tell me to make my bed. I even did the dishes as a kid without being asked because I couldn't bear the site of them sitting stinky in the sink.

So, together, Landon and I drew back his curtains, tidied away all the loose socks and lightning cables, rearranged the furniture, swapped out the curtains and bedding, and repainted the walls. The bedroom makeover was exactly what he needed to get past his slump. Just as perking up his space did the trick for my son, tapping my inner domestic god was therapy for me. During the COVID months, I found great joy in fixing up my new home, repurposing and refinishing old bits of furniture. I also discovered a passion for vacuuming. With Teddy roaming the house, I'm constantly finding little hairy golden retriever tumbleweeds everywhere. So it's become like COVID therapy to get out the ole Dyson V11 Animal cordless vac and suck it all up. I'd be lying if I didn't admit there is sweet satisfaction of a job well done that I bask in after every vacuum session. Do others feel this way, too, or am I the only weird one?

Zipping Up the Mess

The lockdown also forced me to be more creative. I needed to build a sense of real intimacy with the folks I was interviewing without being in the same room. And I needed to transmit that connection to my audience of viewers and listeners. To that end, I had to dig a little deeper in my questions, getting the stars to open up more about the very real and human struggles with what we were all dealing with: the specter of COVID, the fear of getting ill, and, for many, the economic blow of not being able to get out there and earn a living. Again, I peeled back the layers, not so much making it about myself but revealing more about my own life and what I was going through. I got my interview guests to do the same.

Of course, many of us were blessed to still have jobs, security, and the financial means to get through this while social distancing. That wasn't the case for a lot of my listeners, who were unemployed or facing down death every day as nurses and doctors, or dealing with the pain of shuttering a small business and wondering how to put food on the table for their families. But we all shared the same fragile state, facing a health threat that did not discriminate.

This strange moment in history was an opportunity to demonstrate that we were all human, that we were not alone. Rich, poor, young, or old, we were all facing our own mortality. My celebrity guests were just as affected by this as the fans, at least in terms of feeling vulnerable and fearful. We were all going through something huge.

I consider myself a natural empathizer, so the situation played to my strengths as a caring listener who could offer fragments of relatability to anyone on the other end of the conversation. In a crafty way I brought these commonalities up as often as I could in my interviews. Some of the artists I interviewed had been dealing with loved ones who were sick. Others were dealing with career disappointments. In September 2020, ahead of the Academy of Country Music award show, the aforementioned Kelsea Ballerini was once again passed over for a much-deserved nomination. Everyone, including Kelsea, thought she'd be a shoo-in, but, in fact, being passed over is what her song "Homecoming Queen" was all about.

Look damn good in the dress
zipping up the mess
dancing with your best foot forward.

I asked her how she bounced back. How did she make it through the trial of disappointment? How does a person go on in the face of something even more serious, whether emotional or physical?

"I just get up, put one foot in front of the other again, and keep going," she told me. "I look to the next day, and the next thing, and continue to strive to do absolutely the best I can, and that's all I can do."

In It Together

Amen. I feel the same way. Sometimes I have to push myself, even when the baggage is heavy, and I don't even know where exactly I'm headed. That seemed to be the state of the whole country the year of COVID. It didn't matter who we were or what we had, we were all vulnerable.

On the face of it, my life was more than okay. I was conquering the challenge of working in this brand-new way and producing a high-quality show from my house. Who knew? My loved ones were healthy. But then one day in August of the Year of COVID, as Trea and I were driving to the beach to hang out with our family, my heart started beating fast, I felt a pain in my chest, my hands went clammy, and I felt like I couldn't get enough air in my lungs.

"Babe, you need to drive me to the hospital," I told Trea. "I think I'm having a heart attack."

I really thought I might die. They ran all kinds of tests and assured me my heart and lungs were in great condition. "Well then, what was that?" I asked. The doctor said I was having a panic attack. In my head, I'd felt perfectly calm. I thought I'd mastered the whole COVID situation. My conscious mind had it all held together. But I guess my subconscious mind had other ideas. Maybe, as I was keeping myself busy with the show, the house, the family, I wasn't tuning into myself deeply enough. The fact that the love of my life had been on the front line day in and day out for months had to have taken its toll. Of course, I was worried about him! Of course, a part of me was terrified we'd both get infected and become two of the more than half-million casualties of this disaster.

Fast-forward to February 2021, when Trea and I did finally test positive. The brave man had been working in the COVID units of assisted living centers since the beginning of the pandemic, so I knew it was only a matter of time. Bad things happen even when you do all you can to prevent it. He was getting tested every other day and was sent home on a Monday with the news. I made a separate living space for him downstairs in our guest room, and by Tuesday he started having symptoms. By Wednesday I started feeling lousy, waking up with a sore throat, fever, aches, and a cough. That Thursday, I had a Zoom interview with Luke Bryan, so I took some Tylenol and did my best, warning him beforehand that I might not be my usual perky self. I smiled through the interview, and no one knew the difference. Sometimes you've just gotta push through it!

By the next day, my fever was gone. The worst phase of it lasted a week and felt like the flu, except that I lost my sense of taste and smell. And I still get tired running up the stairs. But Trea and I were among the lucky ones.

A week after my interview with Luke, he called to see how I was feeling. That's Nashville for you. Even though I have a working relationship with these artists, it's such a close-knit community. They genuinely care about my well-being, especially Luke. I already knew that to be true, but the year of the pandemic confirmed this.

It's been a mix of blessings and curses. The virus came and left my body, but not the anxiety. I buried myself in projects as a way of coping. But my physiological self wasn't buying it. Just because I had this beast of a situation by the tail didn't mean it couldn't turn around and bite me in the butt. My doctor said he was seeing a lot more patients experiencing anxiety who had never suffered from the condition before. There must have been millions going through similar moments. The condition was something I'd just have to learn to live with and manage. I was troubled by the fact that it comes with no warning, just when I think I am doing great. It was yet another reminder to slow down and pay closer attention to what was going on deep in my soul.

Prayer and meditation have helped me immensely as tools to cope with anxiety. Also, I've learned to be careful with everything I take into my body, especially alcohol. All those years as a Mormon taught me I don't need it, but sometimes it feels pretty damn good to mix a little Tito's in your drink!

In 2020, I also learned how much we need to listen a little closer to each other, as well as to ourselves. My career has kept me running, from city to city, event to event, interview to interview. But for the first time in my life I've been still for an extended period. I needed to turn inward and tune out all the noise, fear, and political strife. I've focused on building a home with those I love.

I've also taken the time to be truly present to my kids, to make sure they are okay not just with COVID, but all the changes in my personal life. I've checked in with Mom more regularly. Although we couldn't meet in person, my nephews taught her how to FaceTime so that we can look into each other's eyes on our mother/son "digital dates." I've found joy in the simple things, like learning new recipes and reading more books: Adam Rippon's *Beautiful on the Outside* and Laurence Leamer's biography of Johnny Carson, *King of the Night*, and Al Roker's *You Look So Much Better in Person*. I also rediscovered *The Golden Girls* reruns and fell in love with *Schitt's Creek*, to create some healthy distance between the news and bedtime.

I missed the specialness of weekends. I missed the fact that I could go anywhere in Nashville—Target or our favorite taco restaurants—and bump into someone I knew. I missed being able to shake hands with strangers, something that was instilled in me as a missionary going door-to-door.

But, as Dolly sang to us, life would be good again. By June, I was already doing some in-person interviews—outside, of course. My first was with Cole Swindell. We sat on stools by a lake in the back of one of our TV producer's homes. Six feet apart looks odd on camera. It looked miles away, and I'm not sure I loved it. The protocols made it awkward. You can't get out of your car until someone comes to get you, and you have to keep your mask on until the artist shows up. Catering consists of individually wrapped sandwiches, and you're lucky if you can get a Capri Sun. Not the usual homecoming party. But it was nice to see the familiar faces of our crew, or at least their eyes above the mask lines.

Ramping up to the awards shows, I interviewed Sam Hunt in September. In preparation, I got a COVID test seventy-two hours before, then twelve hours before. There's a COVID test concierge service that comes to your house, so you can get your nose swabbed in your own driveway, another modern convenience that's come to us by way of a global pandemic. When in-person TV tapings resumed, I started counting the number of COVID tests I'd taken—fifty-six at last count! I honestly don't know if I should be proud of this achievement or not.

And the awards shows did happen after all. For most, only one artist, their band, or a manager was allowed onstage at a time. Not even talking heads like me could get too close. But for the first time since I started my career, I was able to sit back and watch a full award show from the comfort of my couch, live tweeting my thoughts instead of waiting backstage to congratulate the artists and frantically thinking up interview questions in the moment. I could enjoy the presentation almost like a normal fan.

Dierks Bentley's one caveat with our awards show bet was that there had to be a live audience. Well, there was a smattering of people physically present, and millions were watching from their homes in real time, so technically I guess I won. Dierks owes me a suit. The problem is, at the time I'm writing this, I'd be all dressed up with nowhere to go.

• HIGH ON A PEDESTAL •

by Terresa, Cody's ex-wife

THANKSGIVING 2020 WAS SMALL by our standards, with only the closest of family getting together to celebrate; me; my three kids; my boyfriend, Patrick; Cody; Trea; and their dog, Teddy. We packed up all the side dishes, including Patrick's famous mac and cheese, and drove over to Cody and Trea's house, where we hung out on the deck on a sunny, crisp fall day, warmed by a firepit, heat lamps, laughter, and love. The pandemic notwithstanding, it was a typical modern family event for us, with plenty to eat and drink. Cody even got out the slide projector after the sun went down, as we cozied up under extra blankets and looked back on our wonderful history together. Our son, Landon, said it was the best Thanksgiving ever. In spite of all that the world had gone through that year, I never felt more grateful.

A little more a decade ago, if anyone had told me this was how our family would look, I'd have called them crazy. I didn't have the slightest notion that my husband was gay. But when Cody first came out to me, I wasn't angry. I didn't feel betrayed. What I felt was overwhelming grief and frustration, with myself. How could I have missed this huge fact about the most important person in my life? Why couldn't I have listened more, paid attention, and seen this beautiful man for who he really is? I spent a long time beating myself up for being too self-centered while he'd lived all those years suffering in silence. I was mad at God and the world for making my husband feel like he had to hide his light his whole life. From that point on, I was determined that he would not have to go through this alone. Whatever Cody needed, I'd walk this journey beside him.

Of course, it wasn't a sprint to where we are now. We had our moments. But the one thing I never doubted was that Cody loved me deeply, even if it wasn't the passionate, romantic love I felt for him. He was, is, and will always be my person, my soul mate. He has gone above and beyond to take care of me and our children but, more than that, he's never left me emotionally. We are empty nesters now, but Cody, who would do anything for me, has made sure that I never feel alone.

I put him so high on a pedestal that it can be hard for anyone else who comes into my life. They will surely lose by comparison. Of course, I was heartbroken when our relationship as husband and wife ended and it still hurts sometimes. I am working things out on a daily basis. But I would not change any of it because it's helped me to grow and love in ways I never imagined. My life is good now. Cody and I were put together for a reason. I'm here to be that person who gives him unconditional support and understanding. And I believe Cody came into my life in part to show me that love is love, whatever form it takes.

((11))

A DIFFERENT VOICE

We ain't gotta be just alike
And not everything is black or white.
—JIMMIE ALLEN, "All Tractors Ain't Green"

More bad news. Just as we were starting to adjust to this new way of living under lockdown, Nashville got hit with another storm. On May 30, right after the horrifying footage of George Floyd dying as a police officer's knee was on his neck, the glass panes on storefronts, restaurants, and bars up and down our iconic Broadway were smashed. The historic downtown courthouse was set on fire. The Stage, a rowdy country music bar where aspiring artists perform in the hopes of being discovered, was among the businesses that were vandalized and looted. Police cruisers were set on fire and members of law enforcement were targets as rioters threw rocks and bottles at them. What started out as a peaceful rally called "I Can't Breathe" had, by nightfall, been hijacked by an unruly few and devolved into violence and destruction. Similar scenes were playing out in cities across the country.

My reaction to that video of George Floyd's arrest was the same as most people's. I was sickened and stunned. But that unifying moment quickly passed. People turned on each other as anger and outrage took over. It was a culmination of something I'd been noticing over the previous few years.

Us and Them

As a culture, we'd lost the ability to listen. No one was really hearing each other anymore. Our nation had been torn apart by divisive politics, leaving people feeling isolated, angry, fearful, and misunderstood. Just flick on most any cable news show, or talk radio, and all you could hear was people screaming over each other. No one was actually communicating. People were so entrenched in their positions that they were only listening out for perceived insults and ammunition to score points in an argument. And when we weren't drowning each other out with "us and them" semantics, we were totally distracted by technology, which in our pandemic isolation has been a blessing and a curse. Again, people became so focused on their phone and tablet screens that they couldn't even look you in the eye. Many weren't even trying to understand each other.

Heart-to-Heart

Now, I've never considered myself a political guy. Dolly put it best: "People don't want to hear me mouth off about politics." I never want to be a polarizing figure and I don't view it as my role on radio, television, or social media to tell others what to think. I'm more interested in people. I deal with folks one-on-one, as individuals, with the goal of entertaining and informing my audience. When I interview someone, I want listeners to enjoy the journey and come away with a better sense of who these celebrities are as regular people. If, by the end of the conversation, an artist becomes more relatable to his or her fans, I've succeeded.

But it occurred to me that maybe now was the time for a deeper conversation. I wanted to have an extended heart-to-heart with someone about what was happening in our world, to give my listeners and viewers the opportunity to hear someone with a set of experiences and perspectives that may be unlike their own. Whenever we allow someone who is different to speak their truth, it's a gift. It gives us the chance to connect, relate, find common ground, and bridge whatever divides us. My interviewee had to be wise, kind, and honest as the day is long—someone whose humanity shines through every word. I knew just the guy.

I loved Jimmie Allen from the first time we met. A black artist who launched his career with a number one single, "Best Shot," he has quickly became one of country music's finest stars. One of the things I admire most about him was that he truly struggled to make it in our business. The guy did all kinds of odd jobs, training clients at a Gold's Gym and showering where he worked because he slept in his car. He did that for months, working on his music and bouncing between ten different jobs, from assistant youth pastor to salesman at Home Depot.

We were drawn to each other in part because we were both relative unicorns in Nashville. How many black people can you name at the top of the country music food chain? Although Jimmie is straight, he told me early on how much he admired me for coming out as gay. I've interviewed him several times over the years, and they were some of my best conversations. We even talked about doing a podcast together and calling it *Alan and Allen*. Each segment would focus on what it's like to be different, and the judgments and unconscious bias that come along with it. But it wouldn't be all serious. Jimmie, who calls me his "cousin" and was quick to tell me "Bro, forget African American, just call me black," is funny and incisive. No wonder Hoda Kotb asked him to cohost with her on *The Today Show*. Like me, he's not especially political, but he's never afraid to express how he feels, and he never avoids a difficult subject. He slices through all the bullshit with authenticity. He shows up for everyone as a human being, which is why his fan base cuts across all demographics. I mean, how could you not love a guy who's as crazy as Jimmie is about Disney and theme parks?

When we dialed in on Zoom to discuss what was happening in our world, Jimmie from inside his truck and me from my makeshift studio, he didn't disappoint. I began to understand where we are as a society in a whole new way. Hearing him tell it in his own words, openly and honestly, moved me and gave me chills. I, like so many, was stirred by that George Floyd video, but I realized Jimmie had a unique set of emotions that only a person seeing it through his eyes feels and sees.

"So what did you think?" I asked him.

"I pictured my son," he answered, then broke down in tears.

It was at that moment I got it. I was raising a white son, and as a parent I already had plenty to worry about as he grew up and started making his own way in the world. But this was another level of fear that, simply because of skin color, I didn't have to experience. It wasn't fair.

"This guy was getting killed on camera for eight and a half minutes," Jimmie continued. "He was already cuffed, but he had a knee on his neck, and you could see the policeman keep repositioning his knee. What was going on inside this guy's head? How messed up in his heart was he not to see that this is somebody's brother, somebody's son, somebody's friend, that he's purposely taking the life of."

Driving While Jimmie

Seeing it all unfold took Jimmie Allen back to all those times he was treated differently by law enforcement. When "Best Shot" hit number one, he was driving through Virginia and got pulled over for a busted taillight. The officer asked him what he was up to.

"Nothing, sir, I was just on my way home," Jimmie politely told him.

"I don't believe you," the officer told him, "and I may have to ask you to step out of your car."

Right at that moment, another officer pulled up and recognized the country star.

"You're Jimmie Allen, right? You sing that song 'Best Shot.' Man, I love that song!"

Then he apologized for the other officer, pointed out that he needed to take care of that taillight, and sent him on his way.

"But what if that officer hadn't come along?" Jimmie wondered. "What if I hadn't had that hit song?"

As a black man, it wasn't the first or the last time Jimmie felt he came under extra scrutiny or was dismissed out of hand because of how he looked on the outside. Like the time he was walking around one of his favorite mom-and-pop stores in Nashville without his customary cowboy hat and boots. With Jimmie dressed in sweats and a pair of Air Jordans, the manager followed him around the store, repeatedly asking him, "Can I help you?" Meanwhile, Jimmie had noticed a couple of guys "who did not look like me" helping themselves to items on the shelves and stuffing them in their pockets.

"I'm good, like I just told you," Jimmie told the manager. "But those guys are robbing you blind. Are you only asking me because I'm black and wearing a hoodie?"

"Oh no! I'd never do that," the guy protested. Jimmie's point was made.

Racism, in subtle and blatant forms, has been his lived experience, as it has been for many people of color, in ways that can be hard to imagine for those of us who have not walked in their shoes. Nashville has embraced Jimmie, just as the country music world embraced me when I came out as gay. But, even as an artist, Jimmie experienced moments along the way that almost derailed his career and deprived us from witnessing his enormous talent.

Early on, in a meeting, a record label executive told him: "I like you, Jimmie—you're cool for a black guy. But I'm not sure how to market someone who looks like you. I'm not sure how audiences would feel about your people."

Jimmie thought to himself, *Wow, what year is this? Does this guy even realize what he's saying?* Then he walked out in disgust.

Fortunately for us, Jimmie persisted. The radio community and the fans on social media supported him, despite the unconscious and not-so-unconscious biases of the record companies, who somehow overlooked the fact that there are already plenty of artists in country music who happen to be black, from the late great Charley Pride to Darius Rucker, Mickey Guyton, Rissi Palmer, and Kane Brown.

"I see progress, but the old ways of thinking in the industry still exist," Jimmie told me. "And people forget the whole history of country, which came from the blues. Even the banjo originates from West Africa."

A Listening Ear

Jimmie was hurt and angry about what was happening in our country, but he was also compassionate. He was quick to acknowledge that not all people are prejudiced, and that injustices happen to people of all persuasions.

"I am not going to sit here and be naïve. We've all done it. We've all made assumptions. Even as a black man, I can honestly say that, in a threatening situation, I'd rather fight a white guy than a black man. We can be honest and point out our own faults. That's where change starts."

Jimmie was careful about his own judgments. In the days following George Floyd's death, he was pressured by social media followers to say something. Fans wanted him to join in the chorus of outrage.

"But I have to do things at my own speed," Jimmie explained. "When I say something, I want it to be meaningful. I want people to hear my heart. We need to move forward with an open mind and understanding because hateful words don't welcome a listening ear."

Jimmie went on to explain how he tries to examine things from another's point of view. He takes into account how people were brought up, their backgrounds and education. His own parents were raised in different denominations, "and learned things from their parents that weren't in the Bible." A certain belief system had been instilled in them, so they judged the world through that lens. Similarly, when individuals have lived most of their lives in predominantly white communities, don't know any black people as individuals, see them portrayed as criminals on television, and their family tells them to be careful in certain neighborhoods, it's likely they're going to have distorted views about the whole community.

Time to Reflect

"This country has a history of injustice. But the one good thing about being in lockdown is that we've had a lot of time to reflect, to think deeply about what's been happening and what needs to change," I told Jimmie.

We all thought COVID canceled the year 2020 and that we would have to pick it up again in 2021. Instead, it brushed away a lot of the distractions so we could face some truths.

"Maybe this is the year, the moment," he agreed. "I feel like it is."

But we both agreed it had to go beyond words and gestures.

"Don't just post a black square and be part of a social media trend. Don't just say, 'Pray for Nashville.' Are you praying or are you just posting? What's the reasoning behind the posting? Have a plan. Think about whether you are hurting or helping."

Jimmie went on to explain that the real change won't necessarily be seen in the streets. As beautiful as it was to see people of all shades protesting in the streets, blacks and non-blacks shoulder to shoulder, "revolution is what happens in your heart and your mind when it clicks."

But we may not all be on the same schedule.

"When the rest of the world slowly starts to wake up, people have to unlearn what they've been taught and that doesn't happen overnight," Jimmie explained. "We're trying to learn new ways of everyone being equal and having equal rights. We're a lot more alike than we are different. . . . But to change people's hearts, you have to be persistent, passionate, and patient. Everyone learns at a different speed."

Meanwhile, "no matter how you are treated, choose to lead with love and compassion. I had no fan base before country, and since then I have had two hits with support of fans. I'm succeeding in a genre where no one thought someone like me could make it, so I am seeing progress. That love makes it possible to do what you want no matter what you look like or where you are from."

"Good music and good people rise," I said.

When I called on Jimmie, I knew he'd bring a balanced perspective and let love rule, even if that wasn't what some of his followers wanted to hear.

Hijacked Conversation

"People say I should get angry, but what good would that do? Responding with the hate I am trying to preach against defeats the whole purpose. To my Christian friends, how can you love God and not love everyone?"

We talked more about the rioting, vandalism, and looting. We were both dismayed at how a noisy minority hijacked the conversation.

"How do we deal with social justice issues moving forward?" I asked him. "Protest more?"

"When the looting first started and they hit a Nike store, someone said, 'That was us,'" Jimmie joked. "But Sephora, that ain't us breaking them windows with the skateboards! Seriously though, if you want to protest, do it during the day, then leave. Don't do it at night when you are creating camouflage for people trying to terrorize, take for themselves, and disrupt the whole movement."

Good Cop, Bad Cop

Again, like Dolly, I keep any party allegiances to myself. I am for people, not politicians. My conversations with Jimmie are among the few times I am comfortable enough to go there, because I know we're of the same mind and heart.

"If you're going to take action, do it at the ballot box instead," I said.

"Vote for your mayor, your governor, your representative in the Senate," Jimmie agreed. "Vote for someone who is about equality and love for everyone, and who is not going to stand for a police chief who would let that nonsense happen. It's about treating everyone fairly."

For Jimmie, that included individual members of law enforcement.

"Can you support the black community while at the same time supporting good cops?" I asked him.

"Of course! Some of my best friends from childhood are police officers. My cousin is a police officer. They are great people. I don't want to see a black guy treated wrong by one police officer in Minneapolis any more than I want to see a protest where someone throws a brick at an officer just because they think he might be racist. You know nothing about this cop. He could have a black wife and mixed-race kids. That's not how you do it. You shouldn't stereotype cops any more than you should stereotype black people. We need to support blacks, officers, firefighters, Asians, white people. How can I push for BLM if I treat a certain group of people differently?"

Communication *Reset*

At a time when it was extremely unpopular, Jimmie spoke out in favor of balance, patience, and keeping an open mind. He acknowledged his righteous anger about racial injustice and desire for long overdue change. But he would not allow his disappointment to drown out his best impulse: to abstain from reflex assumptions and listen with an open mind and heart. My conversation with Jimmie was like hitting the communication reset button, something we could all use. I listened with fresh ears, and his words made me think back to my own experiences with race growing up in the Deep South.

In high school, two of my best friends were Stacy and Tracy Gregg. They were twin sisters who had the same preoccupations I had at that age: homework, God, and crushes on boys, though not necessarily in the same order. As a teenager well aware of his sexual identity, I may not have looked different from the majority, but by society's standards back then I sure felt different, which could be why I connected with so many minority kids in school. Maybe the fact that I never looked down on anyone was why I got most of the black votes when I ran for student council! My entry into the Mormon Church was another, more visible thing that put me outside the mainstream. But Stacy and Tracy never judged. The Gregg girls even invited me to their black Baptist church on Sundays. I sure loved that feeling of being embraced and accepted. They treated me like family.

New Blood

But that didn't mean there weren't prejudices passed down from generation to generation in the Chavis family. When my sister, Missy, dated a black man and became a teenage mom, my mom and dad were upset. But more out of fear for the way Missy and her child would be treated in small-town South Carolina. In the early 1990s, our part of America was a totally different world, so their concerns were not misplaced. Missy could face name calling or worse. But my grandparents, loving and kind Christians as they were, reacted out of ignorance. At first, they refused to see my sister, much less allow her and her new husband into their homes. They made it plain that they didn't believe in mixed-race relationships and they shunned her for the longest time.

There was no excusing it. I'm sure they wouldn't have been thrilled if a white boy had knocked up my seventeen-year-old sister, but this was racism pure and simple. I was supportive of Missy, and excited for the birth of my new niece or nephew, but I was far from home and pursuing my radio career in Orlando.

Other than encouraging my family to keep an open mind during the occasional phone conversation, there wasn't much I could do to intervene. My heart hurt for my sister more than she knew, because I understood exactly how it felt to love outside the lines drawn for you by society. I just prayed that the older generation would move past their prejudices and come around, for Missy's sake.

Eventually, they did, thanks to Mom's insistence, and intervention.

"It's not your choice to make," she told my grandparents. "The more you pry or demand something, the more likely she'll be to run the opposite way."

It took a few years, and many more family arguments. Finally, Mom had enough. She brought Missy and her family over to my grandparents' house and forced them to get acquainted with their great-grandchildren. Mom knew how hard it was for their generation to readjust their attitudes, but she wouldn't take no for an answer. Of course, as soon as they got to spend time with Missy's beautiful kids, whose veins coursed with the same blood as theirs and whose faces lit up with the same features—Grandpa's eyes and Grandma's smile—they finally softened.

"Babies come, and you learn they are their own miraculous beings," Mom said. "And just as perfect as any other baby."

It goes back to what Jimmie was saying about giving people a chance to grow and thinking of them as you would your own family. My grandparents didn't know better, but they were decent, God-loving people. I did not appreciate the way they were treating Missy and I hated being caught in the middle, but the goodness inside them finally won. It was just a question of exposing them to a different reality and giving them the time and space to open their ears and hear a different voice. Anyone, no matter how long they've lived or what they've lived through, can evolve if you let them go at their own speed, with a few gentle nudges along the way.

(((12)))

COMING HOME

A few months after I'd come out to the world as gay, I saw Carrie Underwood at the Grand Ole Opry. She'd spoken up for me, adding hers to the chorus of industry voices that lent their support, and this was the first time I'd seen her since. She already knew that she'd been an inadvertent Cupid for Trea and me, so when I introduced her backstage to Trea and his entire family—his mom, dad, sister, and brother-in-law—each of whom are huge fans, she could not have been more gracious.

That night we also met her best friend, Ivy, for the first time. Ivy runs the popular cake business Ivy Cakes in Franklin, just outside of Nashville. As soon as she saw us, she gushed: "Oh my gosh, I am so excited to meet you two! Carrie loves you and loves your story after all that you've been through."

It was yet another warm hug from the city I love.

There have been so many other moments of human connection with listeners, colleagues, stars, and regular folks in the crowd since I shared what was in my heart with the world. I had hidden a huge part of myself from these people for so long, it never even occurred to me that I would be wholly accepted as a beloved friend. Before I tuned into my authentic voice, I used to be something of a social recluse outside of work. It was exhausting to be "on" all the time and feel like I was playing a role.

But now I'm not only comfortable running into all kinds of kinds, it thrills me. Wherever I go in Nashville, or any venue in the world where there are country music fans, I walk tall. I don't fear the recognition, I don't shun the exposure, especially because it's an opportunity to have conversations with young members of the LGBTQ+ community who feel safe speaking with me. For example, when I take our shows on the road through the USO and American Forces Network, visiting bases across the globe, I often have members of our military pull me aside to say thanks for coming out. I tell them it wasn't easy, but it sure wasn't as hard as I feared it would be, and now I can't even imagine what it would be like to keep on pretending. Some say thanks because it gave them the courage to do the same. Some seek advice. Others just want to share a beer and a few laughs as we stand together and listen to the music.

There's nothing better than that feeling of connection with other people from all walks of life when you are unguarded and ready to share. Fully listening, to God, to myself, and to others, has fundamentally changed my relationship to the world. I've been blessed to receive an outpouring of support from fans, artists, and members of my industry, as well as the tidal wave of messages from fans who are relieved to see someone they can identify with come out the other side of this feeling happy and free. I came out and the world didn't come to an end. People heard me, loud and clear, and they accepted me. Maybe, just maybe, they can do the same when the time is right for them.

Dust & Debris

Of course, I am still adjusting to my new life as an openly gay man. It doesn't totally define me. I am many other things, including a father, a son, a friend, and a media personality. My baggage is lighter, but I still carry vestiges of guilt for any hurt I've caused people I love for not telling the truth sooner, for not being fully present in the moment as I could have been. Coming out is not like flicking a switch. Interestingly, so many of the friends and family I came out to first said, "I wish you had told me sooner." At least now I've got company. I know that I don't need to go through any of this alone. Having my "tribe" completes the circle.

I am more comfortable in my skin, and more willing to take the leap in many areas of my life, even if that just means letting loose and having more fun. I don't censor myself anymore. Being "out" allows me to interact with others without the constant filter for any signs I might reveal myself. And I can listen in full appreciation, with my guard all the way down, open and ready to receive. Above all, now that I am being completely open and real with my listeners, I'm in a position to help and inspire others who are going through their own struggles.

Being heard as my authentic self has given me the opportunity to connect with folks in a way I never could have imagined before I went on this journey. Now, when I listen, I can respond with my whole heart, and the communication moves freely, both ways. And it goes beyond my inner circle of friends and family. I am touching people who are hearing my story for the first time, and it's emboldening them to let their own voices be heard. They realize that there's more that unites us than divides us, and that if they can find the courage to be bold, they'll find someone to hear them with compassion. Thanks to the art of listening, to myself and to others, I was able to build a support system that could catch me when I finally made that leap.

Live & Loud

Then, well, COVID. No more bear hugs or sloppy kisses with the outside world for any of us, at least for a while. Stuck at home for months on end, I missed my peeps. But love found a way during the filming of the 2020 CMT Awards.

I was onstage in the middle of Cumberland Park, along the riverfront that runs through the heart of Nashville. As I looked up past the lights, cameras, and monitors, I saw them: a crowd of fans, some practically hanging off the Korean Veterans Boulevard bridge, whooping, hollering, and clapping as if they were at an old-fashioned music festival. It was as if the whole town had come to a stop, craning to see what was going on. During the first awards show that year to have a live audience, I was with my CMT cohost, the fabulously talented Katie Cook, along with a few in-person celebrities like Kane Brown, Ashley McBryde, Sarah Hyland, as well as Brooks & Dunn, Noah Cyrus, Jimmie Allen, and Luke Combs, who shotgunned a beer during his opening song, "1, 2 Many."

Don't get me wrong, we weren't breaking the COVID rules. Our venue had been CDC sanitized and approved, with comfy CMT blue and red branded blankets and coolers marking the spot where our two hundred invited guests could sit, stand, or lie down on the grass safely socially distanced, like kindergartners at nap time. My cohosts and I lived in a COVID-free semi-bubble a few days prior, and COVID tested at least twice before the cameras rolled.

It wasn't exactly the party atmosphere, with bar service and snacks, that the CMT Awards show is known for. No friends, family, girlfriends, boyfriends, or spouses were allowed on set, and the crew was one-tenth the size of a regular awards show: a couple of producers, a camera guy, and a sound guy. Backstage, our chairs were six feet or more apart, and we had to wear our masks until the cameras rolled, which wasn't exactly pleasant after having our makeup done, at least for this dude. Normally the event would have taken place in June at the Bridgestone Arena but, like all other award shows in 2020, we had to make a few adjustments.

Many of the performances took place at remote locations throughout the Greater Nashville area, like Ruskin Cave in Dickson County, a soundstage of carved rock and trickling springs with incredible acoustics made by nature. Little Big Town performed "Wine, Beer, Whiskey," with twenty-foot liquor bottles projected onto the cave walls, and images of heavenly trumpet players looking down on the real trumpet players on the stage (maybe that's what Mom was describing in the rapture). Maren Morris performed an acoustic version of her song "To Hell & Back" from an attic in Ashland. Ashley McBryde sang "Martha Divine" from the Barn at Sycamore Farms, with farm tools as stage props, while Luke Bryan sang "What She

Wants Tonight" from his own socially distanced location on an island in the middle of the pond outside the barn.

Not every CMT act and award acceptance speech was streaming in from within the state of Tennessee. Blake Shelton and Gwen Stefani toasted their industry honors from their home in Los Angeles. Kelsea Ballerini and Halsey slinked all over some deserted bar in Hollywood for their duet, "The Other Girl." But for me the highlight of the evening was beamed in all the way from Switzerland by Shania Twain. She sang "Whose Bed Have Your Boots Been Under?" to celebrate the twenty-fifth anniversary of her album *The Woman in Me*, and you could see and hear how much fun she was having camping it up inside the Chaplin's World Museum, saucily playing off the Charlie Chaplin statues. After struggling so long with vocal issues, she was back.

The show was a perfect hybrid of in person and digital; live and pre-taped. It had the kind of energy that was lacking in most of the other awards show across industries and genres. I put that down to our live audience in Nashville, which was the sticky glue that held the whole thing together. We were the first to figure out how to incorporate live audience reactions, and there's just nothing like seeing the faces of fans, or I should say the half faces behind those masks, as they danced, cheered, and clapped in reaction to killer performances on those giant monitors. We coached them beforehand to demonstrate their love, because the success of the show depended on them, and they were happy to oblige, as were the fans hanging from the bridge. We amplified their two hundred voices for radio and television, and the end result of their real-time reactions was seamless. You couldn't even tell that some of the performances had been pre-taped.

The weather could not have been better. Late October brought us an Indian summer. The temperature was in the seventies, with no humidity and a light breeze. We prepped onstage just as the late afternoon sun was hitting the buildings of downtown Nashville with its golden light. We kicked off the show, flooding our grassy makeshift arena with spotlights just as the sun disappeared below the horizon and the skyline lit up in the background.

It felt especially good to be the guy on the scene with the audience. Live television is a pressure cooker, with millions watching and multiple moving parts. Anything can go wrong. Katie and I had to be quick on our feet. I was anxious beforehand, but in the moment, I felt amazingly self-assured. My presentation was crisp, precise, and on point. The performances crackled with extra exuberance. After months of lockdown, it reminded me that this was why I do what I do.

From the fans beyond the park fence to the country stars I have worked with for decades, to the new generation of artists whose time it was to shine, this moment was the culmination of everything I love about this business, what I show up for every day. Although I knew we could be facing several more challenging months ahead, there was a sense that we were finally turning a corner, and I was coming back to the place where I belong. Home.

• ACKNOWLEDGMENTS •

FIRST, THANK YOU TO EVERY single person who has touched my life. I have told many stories here of those who have shown me love and friendship, but not all. You know who you are, and I love and appreciate you. Most especially, I thank those who in some way helped guide the turns that have led me here.

To Keith Urban, who wrote the wonderful foreword to this book, thank you for your friendship.

To my family, thank you for always supporting me in every decision and dream. While "star friends" are all great relationships I treasure, it is my family who makes every moment possible.

To my writing coach/editor/therapist, Samantha Marshall, who helped to beautifully weave my random stories into readable coherence, always keeping my grammar and punctuation in line. Thank you for the pure enjoyment it's been to share with you how best to bring my life to print. I will miss our writing (therapy) sessions.

Thanks to my CMT family also. Without you, many of my adventures never would have happened: Brian Philips, Dingo O'Brien, Curt Miller, Quinn Brown, Leslie Fram, Ashlee Mc-Donald, Lauryn Snapp, Cory Linton, Heather Lee, Keith "Cracker" Durham, Katie Cook, Marley Sherwood, Ashley Sha-hAhmadi, Dustin Stout, Anne Oakley, John Hamlin, Margaret Comeaux, Alecia Davis, Yasmin Mohammed, Ritch Sublett, Libby Mitchell, Michelle Babbitt, and the hardworking Jimmy Corn, who has been with me on every TV shoot I've done over the years. Also, to all the crew people who have ever made me look or sound better than I am, thank you.

Thanks to my media agent, Paul Anderson, whose wicked smartness and keen intuition have helped me navigate my professional climb and my personal journey.

It takes a village or, as I say, a tribe. Friends you can count on, anytime for anything. Thanks to those who answer my calls and texts: Jeremy Young, Chris Swallow, Kelsea Ballerini, Gavin DeGraw, Lee Brice, Gayle King, Patrick Kelly, Jake Owen, Jimmy Miller, Justin Moore, Kelleigh Bannen, Colton Underwood, Gus Kenworthy, Luke Bryan, Jennifer Nettles, Michael Monaco, Jeffrey Nelson, Michael Ray, Jason Deere, Tyler Hubbard, Brian Kelley, T.J. Osborne, John Osborne, Whitney Nevitt, Adley Stump, Blake Kinsman, Jaymes Vaughan, Jonathan Bennett, Lindsay Doyle, Zeke Stokes, Ty Herndon, Tyler Rich, Will Hitchcock, Dave Haywood, Donna Jean Kisshauer, Dan Smyers, Shay Mooney, Molly Young, Jackson Boyd, Unnecessary Grunts, Ryan Vaughn, and Shaun T. And finally, Casey Jones, who gave me the final nudge to write the book, after patiently enduring so many of my stories, saying, "You should write a book." *Oh*, I thought. *Maybe I should?!* And so I did.

Thanks to my radio mentors: Brian Philips, Mike Moore, Smokey Rivers, Paul Williams, Rick Dees, Bob Kingsley, Stacey

Brooks, Tony Thomas, Ryan Seacrest, Steve Reynolds, Jason Pullman, Julie Talbot, Rick Murray, Bobby Bones, Keith Stubbs, Blair Garner, Tracy Chapman, Chris Sommer, Rich O'Brien, John Garabedian, and every DJ and host I've worked with and admired over the years.

Thanks to the LGBTQ+ community, who have buoyed me with your encouragement and love. You've shown me that every human is important. Every human.

Thanks to my literary agent, Alan Nevins, and the entire talented team at Harper Horizon. Andrea Fleck-Nisbet, without your belief in me, my story, and this project, I would not have had the courage to put pen to paper, or fingers to laptop. And, of course, Amanda Bauch, for your loving guidance along the way.

Thank you, country music, for bringing the truth to music like no other genre. Country music is the author of so much of my life. I'm honored to be counted among the Nashville music community. You are my foundation.

And finally, thank you to Trea. You miraculously came into my life at the exact right time, showing me the depth of love I once only dreamed of. I live my life to the fullest thanks to you. I love you.

• ABOUT THE AUTHOR •

CODY ALAN is as beloved by the Nashville stars he covers as he is by country music fans. As host and executive producer of CMT Radio, millions of listeners hear Cody daily on more than two hundred radio stations. On CMT's flagship music show, *Hot 20 Countdown*, his face can also be seen in 90 million homes, making him "Country's Renaissance Man" (*Radio Ink*) and the ultimate host and insider.

Born in Columbia, South Carolina, Cody leapt at the first opportunity to be heard on the airwaves at age fifteen. With a single-minded determination to succeed, he built his reputation as a highly regarded radio host over the next two decades. He has won multiple awards, including being named National On-Air Personality of the Year at the *Academy of Country Music Awards* twice and Best Syndicated Personality by Country Radio Broadcasters in 2019. Cody has worked in all roles in the business, from host to executive positions as operations manager and program director. Additionally, he was a nine-time recipient of the Country Music Director of the Year award during his tenure in Dallas.

Cody has opened up beyond the microphone, allowing many country fans to see themselves in his journey. At the start of 2017, Cody made national headlines by boldly coming out as gay. He partners with GLAAD each year to host The Concert for Love and Acceptance. As part of Nashville Pride, Cody has been an honorary speaker, invited to share his coming out story. Most recently, Cody received the 2020 Vision Award from the Human Rights Campaign for his efforts leading in the LGBTQ+ community.

Cody's support for the military has been a key aspect of his efforts to give back. Over the years, he's traveled around the globe to support the men and women of the armed forces at US military bases in Bahrain, Alaska, Arizona, Washington, South Korea, Florida, and more. With the inclusion of the American Forces Network, Cody's shows are now heard on more than one thousand bases and naval carriers in 160 countries.

The man Keith Urban says "makes Ryan Seacrest look like a slacker," Cody is a proud father of two. When he's not on the air, he enjoys spending time with his partner and family. He was also named one of "Nashville's Most Beautiful People" by *Nashville Lifestyles* magazine.